T0129819

Power of One

Dulcie Anne Callender-Prowell Ingleton

iUniverse, Inc.

New York   Bloomington

iUniverse books may be ordered through booksellers or by contacting:

iUniverse
1663 Liberty Drive
Bloomington, IN 47403
www.iuniverse.com
1-800-Authors (1-800-288-4677)

Because of the dynamic nature of the Internet, any Web addresses or links contained in this book may have changed since publication and may no longer be valid. The views expressed in this work are solely those of the author and do not necessarily reflect the views of the publisher, and the publisher hereby disclaims any responsibility for them.

ISBN: 978-1-4401-8221-1 (sc)
ISBN: 978-1-4401-8222-8 (ebook)

Printed in the United States of America

iUniverse rev. date: 12/15/2009

Power of One is a compilation of thoughts, inspirations, experiential short works and writings. It is a conscientious attempt to make sense of my life experiences in written words and to make meaning of my human actions and interrelationships with people and natural occurrences. It is philosophical in that it presents current thinking and insight of one individual, the importance of one's own view and one's actions within a universal context. It takes a look at what human beings have in common with one another and their existence on earth.

Power of One is something that I would like to share with you. This is my first book and I think you will like it. This book is about you, the individual, who wants to think and have one's own thoughts. It is about communicating one's views, one's convictions. It is about being free to express oneself and to tell one's own story. It is about one woman, one God and one people. In a world where our views are largely shaped by the media or the dominating philosophy of the day, this book is about my inner revelations and personal ideas that have evolved on a daily basis. *Power of One* is my personal journey to enlightenment.

Dulcie An'

This is dedicated to you with love.

Table of Contents

One Short Story

Georgetown, Guyana
1937

That year my mother, Uni, a strapping young woman, brown skinned and high-cheeked, big boned and bow-legged, a real 'thoroughbred' (she said 'tarabred') in stature, had a 22" waistline, was nineteen and beautiful. My mother, Cleopatra Urania Callender, loved to dance and she often told us that when she went to a party there would be at least five young men surrounding her, asking her to dance and because she loved to dance, she would dance with each of them. William Troughmorton Prowell was a fine looking man with dark skin and wavy hair, six years her elder, and quite a lady's man. They both cut striking figures on and off the dance floor. She told me so many stories. Willy would often stand to the side and beckon a 'let's go' to her. She would dance some more. One night after he took her home, he didn't let her go. As usual, she walked him to the door and they would start kissing and Willy, as usual would start 'finggling' her bubbies. As they lay on the floor his hands quickly moved through the crinoline, she breathed out softly, "Willy, Mother is in the back." "Oh girl!" was all she heard him whisper.

Willy, my father, was her first and last man. The next year, 1938, she became Mrs. Prowell and Mommy. She said that the first time she wore a bra was on the day she got married and she made it herself. She made her wedding dress and as a seamstress, outfitted a lot of brides in Georgetown as well. She made most of our clothes and on Sundays we would get dressed up for walks to the Seawall. I remember that. With the help of my grandmother, Angela Callender, who was a nurse and midwife, my mother had six girls first – Claudette, the one that died, Pamela, Bernadette, Paulette and me, Dulcie. We never forget the one that died. Then she had the twins, a daughter, Roxanne and son, Rawn. The three boys, Keith, Patrick and Paul were born in America. When we came to the U.S. she didn't sew too much for us because she liked to make 'pretty' clothes and we didn't like 'pretty' clothes. We became Americanized with the urban wear.

In spite of all the mismanagement, exploitation and underdevelopment that characterizes Guyana, it's a magical place to me. The Temehri Indians believe God was there and made inscriptions on the mountains which they thought no man could make. I have so many fond memories of the rain. When it rained a lot, my father did not go to work and everybody stayed home. When it rained a lot, we didn't go to school and it was so hot, we used to play outside in the rain.

I remember the day my uncles Eustace and Francis got into a fight because I fell over Uncle Francis's foot. Uncle Eustace yelled at him. "You too careless man. You shouldn't have ya foot deh and mek she fall." I remember the classical music on the radio, the contrasting calypso and tramping in the street, their bodies thundering against the wall with plates and tables falling on the floor and their bodies crashing against the furniture in the house. I heard they poisoned the three dogs that bit me and at times I smell the hospital and taste the ice cream I was given after I was bandaged. I still have the dogs' teeth marks on my arms.

My grandmother, Angela Callender

My mother, Cleopatra Urania Callender Prowell and Claudette, her
first daughter

My mother, my father, Claudette, Pamela, Bernadette, Paulette and
me, Dulcie, in my mother's womb

Guyana is my home; I was born there. Guyana is to me, memories, mauby, pepperpot, coconut cake, sorrel, metagee, coo-coo and fish, peas and rice with coconut milk, my mother, and all the sacrifices she made for us, my aunts Bybe and Yvette, her big bottom, her husband Nigel, his brother, Wordsworth McAndrew, the poet, Brickdam Cathedral, the man who used to go to the red woman up Camp Street to get spanked, riding through the burial ground to the housing scheme where we moved to and the window in the bathroom (yes we had a bathroom) that I used to look out at the landscape, the Kaieteur Falls which I have never seen, the gold and diamonds, Nen-Nen and Dada, Daddy Isaacs, Uncle Alfred, the tailor whose wife, Ruth, shot him just because he looked too hard at another woman, Aunt Sheila, who used to put extra meat under my Uncle Eric's rice before they got married, Aunt Evril whose son died in California of a drug overdose, my family, all of them in New York, Texas, Canada and Israel. All of them have a little Guyana in them and this is a story about all of us.

We are going to America.

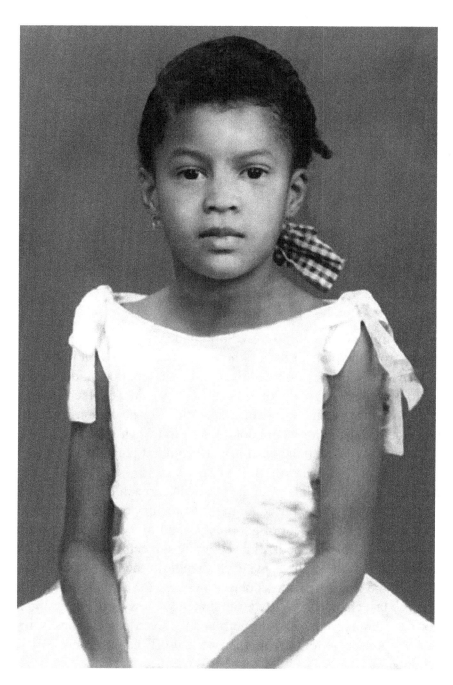

Dulcie, at seven, 1957

Brooklyn, New York
1957

The lights coming into New York made the biggest impression on me from the plane. I didn't know then that those light bills had to be paid to Con Edison monthly, that those American kids would try to beat the 'kungx' out of us because they said we talked funny, that those three white boys would spit at me for no reason and that nun would slap me for what I don't know and when I started to cry, she would try to keep me quiet and we couldn't play outside in the rain. I went to St. Martin of Tours parochial school; it was near Knickerbocker and Halsey, in the Bushwick area of Brooklyn. Not all the nuns were bad. I used to go to the rectory on Saturdays and they would give me a lot of good cakes and bread and pastries to bring home. I liked school, did well in my subjects and managed to graduate from the eight grade even though in the last week, three of us in the graduating class played hookey, for a whole week. It was our last chance to go to the automat downtown, ride the trains, go the Highland Park and do nothing. We even played hookey in Sugar's house; we told her mother we had off that afternoon from school.

That Friday when I turned the corner and saw my mother standing outside the house, I knew she knew. What made us think that no one would find out? Stupid and young, that's what. I started crying from the top of the block on Bushwick Avenue to the middle of Jefferson Avenue where we lived. I cried so much I didn't even get a beating that day. Debbie feigned an asthma attack and she got off. I don't know what happened to Sugar because she didn't speak to me after that. It wasn't only my fault. Anyway, before the hookey incident, Sugar and I were inseparable. On Saturdays, after my sisters and I cleaned the house, Sugar would come over and then we would start doing our hair. We went to the same high school but she avoided me and I still feel bad about not being able to share our high school years together but she was white so I was made out to be the bad one. We all agreed to play hookey one day and then each succeeding day we couldn't figure out a way to go back together - we were in the same class. After that, I never played hookey again.

I have had a good life. I have been working since I was twelve. I used to help two Jamaican boys, Michael and Owen Morris, next door with their homework every day after school and I used to get paid $3. a week and I always had money. I thought I was rich. I always saved and I always remember dressing well. My first big job was with the Neighborhood Youth Corps, working with youngsters in summer programs. I earned about $37. a week and had enough money for school clothes in the fall. I never went to summer school. I made sure I passed my subjects and I worked every summer. My father got up every morning, took a bath, and went to work for the City of New York in Highway Design. My mother was a homemaker and always worked. We always had something to eat; my mother could make something out of nothing. I remember she babysat for Mimi, a little Haitian girl and Mimi's mother paid her $15. a week. In the summers, when we were home from school, my older sisters took care of us and my mother worked in the factory sewing. When I got older, my mother looked at my kids while I worked. From the time my daughter Saba was six months old, my mother kept her and she would only take $35. a week from me and my daughter was there all week. My husband Carl and I would pick her up on the weekends. When she started to get too fat, I took her from my mother and put her in a baby-school. She was so smart.

I went to Bushwick High School after the hookey incident. I didn't want to go to Catholic High School anyway. I told my mother she wasted money sending my sister, to Bishop Loughlin; she became Jewish and lives in Israel with her husband and thirteen children. One of her sons was killed in the park; he was shot in the back of the head and died. I love my sister but the only problem I have with her is that she did not tell me my God's name. The Jewish people know God's name and I read they whisper it in their synagogues. Why whisper? I know a lot of people if they knew or believed in God's name they would want to tell everybody. I can't figure that out and I still don't know why they do that or maybe I know why but I am not going to say it here. Later on I found out. My son, Ossawa, told me My God's name is Yah. He searched out God himself. I always thought about God. I never liked going to church. There was a park right across the street from St. Martin of Tours and there was where I used to spend my church time, outside with nature. Maybe that's why I believe God is the Universe and everything in it. No man created the world. It just is the way It is.

I had great teachers at Bushwick. Ms. Frenette was my English teacher and she always told the class, "Think about what you want to say and say it." She is an inspiration in my life. I remember my history teacher Mr. Plotkin who gave us a weekly exam. I thought that was the best preparation for the final. I think I made a 90% grade in history. He covered the topics in class and reinforced it with the test that was not really hard to study for because it was done in small parts. I liked him. My teacher, Ms. Krausman taught Music. I sang solo at my High School graduation with my brother. You are probably saying how I could do that when my brother was there. My brother is a powerful singer but that night, he couldn't sing; he was stagestruck. I sang by myself. Later in life he became a Muslim and I though maybe that was why he couldn't sing the *Sanctus* at graduation - protest - whatever. Religion does color the way you do things.

Dulcie, graduation at seventeen, 1968

Bushwick was the best High School for me. I didn't have to take Gym if I participated in the Dance Program and that was what I did. My sister, Paulette and I were the "dance stars" in Bushwick. We choreographed and danced to Nina Simone's, *Four Women* for assembly in Bushwick. If you haven't heard Nina Simone sing that song, I can tell you what it's about. It is about being Black, being enslaved and being alive in America. You can just imagine how we communicated this love and anger to students in the assembly hall. I can't forget my dance instructors, Ms. Montague, Ms. Cummings and Helen Weinstein. When Ms. Weinstein jumped into the gym at Bushwick and led us across the floor in some of the most intricate dance patterns, I knew that this was what I wanted to do. This time was in the Sixties and in the Sixties, it was all about Love and love beads and Peace and Black is Beautiful and the Panthers and the Battle of Algiers and going to see the film, *Battle of Algiers*, and the East and music, Martha and the Vandelles, Smokey Robinson, R&B and all that Jazz, especially *Cristo Redemptor* by Donald Byrd, Lee Morgan, *The Sidewinder*, Sarah Vaughn and everybody good. I had a part-time job working at Western Electric and when I graduated from Bushwick, I had a full-time job there. Life was beautiful and I was young and beautiful. Then Martin Luther King died and the reality of America set in.

I left Western Electric. At 20, I was promoted to head the typing pool of about six white girls who had no respect for me or my position. I didn't like correcting their work, covering for their errors and wasting my time with inept supervisors who did not support my position. I started working at New York University.

New York, NY
1970 - Beyond

I started working at New York University in 1970 and while I was there studied dance and dance education. It took me almost 20 years to get a Bachelor of Science in Dance Education. I worked full-time at NYU which allowed me the advantage of tuition remission. I didn't have to pay for my courses, only the registration fees and books. I attended college part-time, after work, on weekends, on my lunch break and worked full time. By the time I graduated, I was in my forties and my life had taken on a new direction. I was married with three children, Saba, Ossawa and Addis. My husband, Carlton B. Ingleton was an artist and we founded what I think was the first Black owned and operated not-for-profit cultural organization in Crown Heights, Brooklyn. I served as the Executive Director of the organization and administered cultural arts and exhibitions programs for a while before I decided to leave NYU in 1983 and work with him full-time.

The organization, 843 Studio-Gallery, was successful in bringing the works of world-renowned artists, such as Romare Bearden, established artists, Otto Neals, Miriam Francis and emerging artists, photographers and writers to the Crown Heights community. While working full-time at the Gallery, I continued my studies and took a loan to finish up my last year of study at NYU. I pride myself in

Carlton and Dulcie at 843 Studio Gallery

Dulcie at Gallery opening in 1981.

knowing that I managed to complete my studies at NYU without compromising my integrity and my ideals. I could have easily lost myself among the predominantly white students there. I was not supposed to attend college. Bushwick High School prepared me to work in the business sector. I had my first math and biology courses at NYU and it was very hard for me. Sometimes I would have to read the assignments three and four times before I could understand what I had to do but I never gave up. If Martin Luther King didn't die, I probably would not have been given the opportunity to study. After his death, there was a move toward appeasing Blacks (we were mad about him and angry that he was taken away) through affirmative action and I took advantage of the educational benefits. In the early seventies I was often the only person of color in my class and a lot of students did not even want to talk to me but that didn't bother me because I didn't want to speak with them either. I got along.

As I grew, I became more interested in art and culture and after administering cultural program in Crown Heights, Brooklyn, came back to NYU in 1994 to work and study, and obtained a Masters in Visual Arts Administration. I still work at NYU at the Law School as a Legal Assistant in the Clinical Law Center and I enjoy my work. My interest in art and culture has developed and my aspirations are to keep myself and my community culturally informed. This is why culture is so important to me. Culture is all about us and the best of what we do as human beings. Too often we are judged by our worst. One of the last projects I worked on was an informative and enlightening art exhibition of works by several talented and skillful Caribbean artists, Kennis Baptiste, Carlton Murrell, Stanwyck Cromwell, Lincoln Perry, David Wilson, Emile Morrison, Anthony Bonair, Winston Huggins and Robert Reid. This art exhibition entitled, EX POSITION - *Out of the Caribbean, Out of this World,* staged in Florida in June, 2008 was one of the most impressive expositions of the African cultural continuum and visually stated in printed, painted, photographic and sculptural images how artists, by recording our life experiences, make meaning of our existence.

So here it is, a brief life story of who I am and what I do. I believe we all have a responsibility to ourselves and each other to do the best we can as individuals to make this world a better place and I think I have done my share of community work, volunteering, promoting and advancing our interests the best way I know how by communicating certain truths about myself, ourselves and aspects of our culture.

Searching for Self

Introduction

The Reality

Where does one look to find out about oneself if there is no record that identifies one's place of origin? I know I am a Black woman. I know I was born in Guyana, South America in 1950 and I have been living in the United States of America since I was seven years old. From where did I originate? Did I come originally from East Africa or West Africa? Am I a descendant of Kings, Queens, or Hebrew slaves?

This is called the year of 2009 and over two thousand years ago people of Africa were exiled, deported and eventually scattered across the earth to satisfy the rich and powerful thirsts for their land and labor. This system called slavery, and its accommodating systems of oppression, forced people into situations to which they had to adapt and in the process, lost touch with their own identities, customs, and cultural upbringing.

Where would you go to find yourself, your homeland, the language you spoke, the foods you ate, how you entertained yourself and the company with whom you came into contact? Begin by acknowledging that something is missing from your identity and that you want to find it. What am I looking for? I am searching for links to the truth of my existence and I learned that sometimes you don't have to look very far to find what you are looking for.

I remember one night I was watching *Jeopardy*, an educational game program on television and the question was what 'bubbie,' a word of Hebrew origin, meant. Well, it meant grandmother. I remember my mother, Cleopatra Urania Callender Prowell, using this word to mean 'breasts' and after a little sequencing, found these words held similar meanings, for example, grand mother, mama, grand mama, and mammary all share the same attributes. This was very significant to me in terms of my identity. As I said earlier, I was born in Guyana and I thought 'bubbie' was a Guyanan word. I spoke with someone the other day whose background is similar to mine. Haile, was born in Grenada and grew up in Trinidad and he is also familiar with this word 'bubbie' and its usage. This means to me that because my mother used this word that it was part of her culture and that because that word is used in cultures similar to mine, that we share evidences of Hebrew language usage. I have also seen pictures of my grandmother, Angela Callender, dressed very conservatively with her head hatted or covered, long sleeves, neck and knees covered and she and my sister named Roxanne, who lives in Israel and who barely knew each other, have similar tastes and exhibit modesty in style and disposition. These little clues are very meaningful and give me some insight into my cultural history.

Some of the principles that were promoted in my family life also bear testament to beliefs that I share with people from similar backgrounds. We were brought up not to take advantage of anyone and not to allow anyone to take advantage of us. These people – my mother and my grandmother – must have been inspired to hold on to these principles, to pass them on to us and I want to look further for indicators to strengthen my belief in who I am.

In my search for self, I find I had to read and one of the books that I found a lot of information in is *From Babylon to Timbuktu* by Rudolph Windsor. The writing was very straightforward and said very plainly and in certain terms, that Black people are the original inhabitants of the world and that Black people have the most ancient history of all humans. To find out more about myself, I would have to begin at the beginning. I found a lot of information in that book and on the internet. If there is anything here that you don't agree with or if you don't believe what I say, you can search for yourself. Information came to me through publications such as *National Geographic*, which I subscribe to, magazines, newspaper articles, and publications in general. What follows is what I learned through research.

I also found that I received information in my mind and I call those revelations or prescripts. I tried to keep my writing as scholarly as possible, citing information to support my views. I decided to include my experiential findings because I couldn't separate my inner experiences from my outer discoveries. What follows is an attempt to 'tell it like it is,' incorporating all of my experiences in a manner in which I feel comfortable. I realized I was writing for my own understanding and that could not be compromised in any way by engaging in matters that I couldn't fully comprehend. I am searching for the truth – whatever it is. I am trying to keep it real.

I am going to start by asking questions and recording instances that would serve to clue me in my search. I am going to find out a little about my ancestors, and their way of life to see if their lifestyles were similar to mine and if we shared the same cultural upbringing. I am going to look at the slave system and trace its progression or digression from Africa to the Americas. I am going to investigate the influences that took away my identity and why. Finally, I am going to arrive at some conclusions based on what I've learned.

I am on a journey. Come with me!

High Order

God & Eve
Adam
Adam & Eve
Man & Woman
Prescript 03/17/2006; 5:02am

<u>In the Beginning ...</u>

Black people have the most ancient history of all humans.[1] Eve, the name given to the first woman on earth, is a name of Hebrew origin meaning 'life.' Scientists now calculate that all living humans are related to a single woman, "a mitochondrial Eve," who lived roughly 150,000 years ago in Africa, and that all of humanity is linked to Eve through an unbroken chain of mothers.[2]

Humans spread from East Africa to the Near East some 80,000 years ago. *National Geographic*, in its March, 2006 issue reveals that

1   Rudolph R. Windsor, *From Babylon to Timbuktu, A History of the Ancient Black Races Including the Black Hebrews,* "Ancient Black Civilization," Exposition Press: New York 1969 (second printing 1973) p. 13.
2   James Shreeve, "The Greatest Journey Ever Told – The Trail of our DNA," *National Geographic*, March 2006, p. 62.

people walked as early as 70,000 years ago from Ethiopia, headed east and traversed the planet. They headed further to southern Asia and Australia some 60,000 years ago, northwestwards into Europe and eastwards into Central Asia some 40,000 years ago and further east to the Americas about 15,000 years ago.[3] There is evidence to support that all of the variously shaped and shaded people of Earth trace their ancestry to African hunter-gatherers.[4] This is supported by the genetic diversity of the African population to produce the physical variations in human characteristics and colors ranging from blue-black to white, the condition known as albinism which prevents the reproduction of color. The new scientific generic information derived from the Human Genome Project, an international effort to decode the information embedded in the human genome, confirmed to the world by scientists in the East Room of the White House, in June 2000:

> "We all evolved in the last 100,000 years from the same small number of tribes that migrated out of Africa and colonized the world. All human beings are 99.99% the same at the DNA level and the remaining 0.1% genetic variation that exists seldom segregates in a manner that confirms to the racial boundaries constructed by social political means."

Dr. Frances Cress Welsing in her book, The Isis (Yssis) Papers, writes about people and color.

> White-skinned people came into existence thousands of years ago as the Albino mutant offspring of black-skinned mothers and fathers in Africa.[5]

There were colonies of albinos formed which eventually migrated northward to the area of the world known as Europe to escape the intensity of the equatorial sun of the Southern hemisphere.

> "The Ice Age had the practical effect of isolating this _____ marginal group from other populations for a prolonged

---

3   http://en.wikipedia.org/wiki/Prehistory.
4   *Id.* note 2.
5   Frances Cress Welsing, *The Isis (Yssis) Papers,* Third World Press: Chicago 1991, p. 23.

period, promoting a consanguinity that would have allowed the recessive albinoid genes to express and propagate themselves…. Albinoid mutation seems as good a speculation since the fossil data and genetic data both seem to rule in favor of a common, Black African ancestry for all mankind."[6]

Postscript:

Color is a visible indicator of one's ancestry and it is a marker that traces among other physical characteristics the origin of human beings. Color is a good thing. You can read more about color in the Isis Papers. You can also read more about albinism and how it is being addressed in our culture. Dr. Ivan Van Sertima in his Anthology of African Civilizations analyzes the conditions which changed the physiology of Black people to embody so called "white" features. I touch on it briefly in the quotation above regarding the Ice Age and the climatic conditions that caused notably the variety of strains that structured the lines of certain eyes, and the streamlining of facial characteristics.

Personally, I feel proud to know that my color is an asset and that this is the way I was designed to be. This knowledge connects me to the source of my being. I know that my color is what makes me unique and that it is a quintessential element that makes me who I am.

The prescript is part of my thoughts or revelations that relate to the topic. I call them prescripts because when the thought comes into my mind, I have to write it down and most of them were written down before this writing. What was significant to me was that when I looked up Eve in the dictionary, it inherently means 'before.' I do not know how the first man or woman was created. I am saying it was a thought that came to my mind and that it had a profound effect on me and that I had to write it down. I could not deny it and when I think about it, it makes sense to me in many ways especially in light of the "Eve" link.

---

6 www.stewartsynopsis.com/chapter_7.htm

"Where Did I Come From?"

The East

Mesopotamia - The Land Between the Rivers

The African Continent was at one time a gigantic land mass, four times the size of the United States. Mesopotamia is commonly known as the 'cradle of civilization.' The land called "Kalam," was situated between the Tigris and the Euphrates rivers. Kalam is a Sumerian word. The land was also known as Ethiopia - Cush (Kush). Mesopotamia was the 'cradle' and Sumer was the 'crib.'

The People and the Land

The people of Sumer (ca. 6000 BCE; [Summer]), are recorded as the earliest known civilized people of the world. Sumerians called themselves *sag-gi-ga*, "the black-headed people," and their land *ki-en-gir*, "land of the civilized lords." Sumerians were Ethiopians, people of color who originated in Ethiopia, in the lower part of the Tigris-Euphrates valley. This area, situated in what was known as Ancient

Mesopotamia, in the most fertile region of Southern Mesopotamia, is now known as the Middle East. Its canals and lakes provided ample irrigation to enliven and refresh this area called, the Garden of Eden, a richly cultivated land grounded with lush trees, fruits, herbs, flowers and vegetation. This area now is known as Iraq and Ethiopia is now situated in what is called, East Africa.

Sumerians were the pre-Semitic population of the lower Euphrates valley. The people who resided in the lower part of the Tigris-Euphrates valley were Ethiopian, black in complexion. They farmed the lands in this region that were made fertile by deposits of the Tigris and the Euphrates rivers. Sumerians were Eastern Ethiopians and they settled along tracts from Mesopotamia to India. There is a blood relationship between the Ethiopian Sumerians and the Dravidian tribes of India. The ancient nations of Sumer, Babylon, Akkadia, and Chaldea were inhabited by Cushites, Ethiopian tribes on all sides of the Tigris and Euphrates rivers.[7] The Ethiopian Empire encompassed the Kingdom of Sheba which was in what is now called Southern Arabia and included Upper Egypt, Ethiopia and parts of Arabia. It was one empire, Sheba (Saba) and Ethiopia to the south of the Land of Israel.[8]

---

7   *Id.* Windsor, note 1, p. 16.
8   *Id.* Windsor, note 1, p. 38.

The Great Tradition

"Our forefathers left us a heritage of a written alphabet, of which we are all today proud benefactors. It is our cherished hope that this historic heritage will pass to generations to come."

His Imperial Majesty Emperor Haile
Selassie I of Ethiopia

Sumerian civilization is substantiated by its art, architecture, astronomical discoveries and social structures. Before writing, culture was transmitted by an "oral tradition" of story-telling, songs, and verbal communications that were passed on. Sumerians developed their language and invented, ca. 4000 BCE, a creative style of writing, *cuneiform*, a system of making meaning by grouping signs developed from pictorial hieroglyphics which predated Egyptian hieroglyphics by at least seventy years. Writing was scripted on clay tablets and formed the basis of their "written tradition."

The English alphabet is derived from two ancient black nations – the Phoenician-Canaanite alphabet and the Hebrew. The first two letters of the Phoenician and Hebrew alphabet are Aleph and Bet. The Phoenicians gave Greeks the alphabet; the Greeks passed it on to the Romans and the Romans to German-Anglo-Saxons. Phoenicians are credited which distributing the phonetic sounds to their linguistic vocabulary. The Creation epic, the *Enuma Elish*, considered to be the earliest writing in Babylonian history, featuring two primary gods, one male and one female, and *Genesis*, in the Hebrews Old Testament of the Bible share a similar creation story. King Hammurabi was famous for his set of laws, The Code of Hammurabi, one of the earliest sets of laws found and one of the best preserved examples of this type of document from ancient Mesopotamia.[9] Hammurabi also instituted the observance of the Sabbath which was adopted by the Hebrews. (The King list representing the dynasties that spanned over five thousand years is too long to list here.) The Ten Commandments, the foundation of the spiritual, moral code which was given to the world by Moses, a black Hebrew liberator, is part of the great written tradition. The Nguzo Saba, the Ethiopian principles which form the basis of Kwanzaa, a world-wide celebration of Afrikin cultural heritage, is part of this great tradition.

Sumerians believed in a primary God, An, the God of Heaven, as well as many gods, such as Anu, the Sumerian God of the sky, and the goddess Ki. An-Ki, is the Sumerian word for universe. Their religious beliefs were polytheistic and varied from one region to another. Kings who ruled over city states were likened to gods. Gilgamesh, a King of Sumer, was considered two-thirds God and one-third human.

The ziggurats were some of the world's first great architectural structures built by Sumerians. These temple platforms which became larger and taller as time progressed reached heights of up to seventy-five feet high and bases of one hundred and fifty feet by two hundred feet. Priests climbed to its top to worship.[10] The Sumerians' painted images, portraits in marble and gray-black diorite and ornate sculptures that adorned their temples reveal great skill and artistry.

Among the inventions Sumerians contributed to world technology are, the wheel, cuneiform, arithmetic, and geometry, irrigation systems, Sumerian boats, lunisolar calendar, bronze, leather, saws, chisels, hammers, braces, bits, mails, pins, rings, hoes, axes, knives, lancepoints, arrowheads, swords, glue, daggers, waterskins, bags,

9   http://en.wikipedia.org/wiki/Mesopotamia
10   http://Art and Architecture, sumerart.htm

harnesses, armor, quivers, scabbards, boots, sandals (footwear), harpoons and beer. Their mathematical prowess led to the invention and development of a sexagesimal system which became the standard number system in Sumer and Babylonia. Using this system, they invented the clock with its 60 seconds, 60 minutes and 12 hours, and the 12 month calendar which is still in use today.[11] The Sumerian calendar measured weeks of 7 days.

"When one speaks of Black Jews, Hebrews, or Israelites, one could be referring to any number of groups. Each is unique, has its own history and follows its own set of traditions. The best, yet most problematic, generalization that can be made about us is that by the prevailing standards of "race," we are all considered black...."[12]

<u>The Hebrews</u>

Hebrews, "people of the land," are an ancient people who lived a nomadic lifestyle and traveled from place to place in search of water, food and pastures for their livestock. Hebrew is not only a language. Hebrew identifies a person who is of a particular place rooted in the land of Ethiopia, and a people who share a consanguineous identity with a lively force of nature who is called Yah.

Hebrew, or Eastern culture, influenced much of the thought and was a major force in the way people perceived the world. Hebrew man was secure with his trust in a spiritual entity who provided support for his existence. Philosophically, Hebraism is a concept of morality and beliefs of a person of faith who is passionately committed to their own mortal being.[13] The concept of an immaterial soul separate from and surviving the body is common today but was not fully founded in ancient Hebrew beliefs.[14] The ancient Hebrews had no idea of an immortal soul living a full and vital life beyond death, nor of any

11 http://www.Sumerian_civilization.htm
12 *Shalom*, Black Jews, Hebrews, and Israelites, members.aol.com
13 William Barrett, *Irrational Man*, Doubleday & Co., 1958, pg. 12.
14 James Tabor, *What the Bible Says about Death, Afterlife, and the Future*.

resurrection or return from death. Human beings, like the beasts of the field, are made of "dust of the earth," and at death they return to that dust.[15]   The Hebrew word for soul is *'nephesh'* and it literally means the "complete life of a being" though it is usually used in the sense of a "living being,"[16] a breathing [creation]. The Hebrews believed that after death, the soul lasted for a brief time in Sheol, a House of Dust and eventually did not exist. There was no conception of an end of time or history, or of a world beyond this one.[17]

Hebrews brought up the belief in one God. This Hebrewism is expressed in African spirituality and it is more pronounced in the first of the Ten Commandments, "You shall have no other gods before Me."

> The African understanding of God was that it was the only and all-in-one energy force that created and simultaneously was all energy in the universe. This understanding recognized the God force as the source of all, the being responsible for all and the multiplicity of energy configurations in the universe. Furthermore, the belief held that there are no energy configurations in the universe that are not from God and that are not God.

> It was the African way to respect completely this source of all energy manifest in and responsible for all things. This is African spirituality. Spirit is energy. Spirituality is the ability to get in touch with, not only the ultimate source of all energy, but also the various multiplicity of energy configurations, which include matter, plants, animals, etc. This was for Africans, the essential cosmic connection-the power connection.

> Since *melanin* is a superior absorber of all energy, it is essential to establish this understanding of God.[18]

---

15 Genesis, 2:7; 3:19.
16 http://en.wikipedia.org/wiki/Nephesh
17 http://www.wsu.edu/~dee/HEBREWS/POSTEXRE.HTM
18 Frances Cress Welsing, *The Isis (Yssis) Papers*, Third World Press:Chicago 1992, p. 171.

Hebrews believed that the world is governed solely by God, Yahwey, and that evil in the world is solely the product of human actions. The Ten Commandments indicates not what the Hebrews did but what they were commanded to do. Moses, the black Hebrew liberator is responsible for revealing to the Hebrews their God, Yahwey, YHWY, Yahuwah, and their way of life, [Yahway]. The Ten Commandments, the moral/spiritual code is famous for outlining the way of life as prescribed by the inspirations of Moses who is not only credited with enlightening the Hebrews to this way of life but the world.

Postscript:

I found I came out of a land and a people who have a great culture. That it was the first of its kind in this world is something I readily identify with and I am proud to know of what my ancestors contributed to the world and its culture.

Unless otherwise noted, I supplied brackets around certain words and text to clarify my understanding.

"What Happened?"

A Lot

The Flood

The flood was a major catastrophe. The biblical report is recorded in the Hebrew Old Testament from the beginning of Genesis to the story of Noah and the Flood and this purging is interpreted as a punishment from "God" for people's sins. Most religious liberals regard the flood as a myth.[19] Whether one believes that God caused the flood to punish sinners or not, there was a flood and although the timing varies as to this world-wide event, most sources say it occurred some time before 2000 BCE. There is physical evidence that proves there was a flood and it changed the landscape of the world. For example, there are billions of fossils buried in sedimentation ("laid-down-by-water rock") found all over the earth. Geologist Dr. John Morris explains:

> "Sedimentary rocks, by definition, are laid down as sediments by moving fluids, are made up of pieces of rock or other

---

19 *Notes*, Religious Tolerance, Important Dates in Ancient Hebrew History, 2009.

material which existed somewhere else, and were eroded or dissolved and redeposited in their location."

Geologists find fossilized trees buried at all angles upside-down and right-side-up often passing through multiple rock layers, obviously the result of a marine cataclysm. These layers of fossils are a world-wide phenomenon. There are also abundant clusters of marine life found atop every mountain range in the world.[20] There are literally hundreds of Flood traditions which have been preserved through the world, Africa, Asia, Europe, Australia, and the Americas which corroborate the biblical Flood account.

Migration

After the flood, the rising salinity led to evaporation of irrigated waters which left salts in the soil making agriculture difficult. People were forced to explore their outer world in search of sustenance for themselves and their tribes. The people who survived the flood, were on a mission to repopulate and rebuild cities. Over centuries, the growth of populations caused people to travel in search of livelihoods for themselves and their families. They developed languages within their own groups and means of communicating within their families and tribes. Travel increased on the seas due to the necessity to explore and find habitable land.

Abraham, a nomadic herder and a native of Sumer was the founding father of the Israelite nation, and a black man. He migrated to Canaan (now known as Israel) where Phoenicians, Amorites and Israelites, who were all called Canaanites lived. Abraham migrated with his tribe from Canaan to Egypt after the flood, after 2000 BCE. Hebrews emerged a dominant presence in Egypt serving the Egyptian Pharaohs by their labors, building their temples and pyramids and working like slaves. They were eventually led out of their servitude by Moses into Israel.

The Phoenicians were ship builders and navigators who traveled to far-away lands by sea and circumnavigated the world. These people

20 *The Flood, The Evidence*, www.allaboutcreation.org. 2009.

established migration and trade routes and immersed themselves in ship building, exploring and seeking outposts for trade and commerce. Ancient Hebrews reached the Americas before Christopher Columbus and set down the Ten Commandments on stone in Hebrew script. This find, along a dry creek bed in New Mexico, is one of the most amazing archaeological discoveries in the Western Hemisphere. Explorer, Gene Savoy, found three stone tablets bearing inscriptions similar to Phoenician and Hebrew hieroglyphs while exploring the ancient civilization of the Andes. It is now common knowledge that ancient Hebrews migrated from Mesopotamia to Mesoamerica and brought their culture with them. This discovery links early Hebrews at the beginning of civilization in Sumer and ties these ancient Black people to the forebearers of the Ethiopian-African cultural continuum in North and South America. There is physical evidence of a black presence in the Maya of Mexico. The Maya, precursors to the Olmec, Aztec and Inca populations, are visually depicted in paint, stone relief and sculpture; their temples, monumental buildings, pyramidal structures and ziggurats, the architectural structures built by their ancient, kindred Sumerians, are visible as well, throughout the western hemisphere.

> "An overwhelming body of new evidence," says Professor Ivan Van Sertima, "is now emerging from several disciplines, evidence that could not be verified and interpreted before, in the light of the infancy of archaeology and the great age of racial and intellectual prejudice. The most remarkable examples of this evidence are the realistic portraitures of Negro-Africans in clay, gold and stone unearthed in pre-Columbian strata in Central and South America." [21]

Invasions

Mesopotamia included Sumer, Akkadia, Babylonia and Assyrian empires. Sumer was ruled by King Sargon and called Akkadia. His empire stretched from the Mediterranean to the Persian Gulf. Sumer

---

21 Professor Ivan Van Sertima is the author of *They Came Before Columbus*.

was called Babylon after the "confusion of tongues," which resulted after an admonition by "God" to deter the building of idols and idle worshipping was not obeyed. *Babel*, a word meaning confusion in Hebrew, is the eponym from which Babylon or Babylonia, the name given to this region in Southern Mesopotamia was derived. Sumer was called Assyria from Assur, the city's patron deity. Mesopotamia experienced the colonization of their land by foreign powers, namely, Europeans and Indo-Europeans. There was a proliferation of languages in Babylon after the land was invaded by people speaking in different tongues. There was a German European invasion of the 'Middle East' sometime after 2000 BCE and the Germans intermingled with the people and established a presence there. [Yiddish, a language spoken by many Eastern-European Jewish people, is a conglomerate of German and Hebrew.] During the second millennium BCE, Persians, Indo-Europeans, invaded the Middle East and mixed with black Asiatics as far away as India. The names of these empires change but the geographic location remains the same, initially, the land of Ethiopia, the Garden of Eden, Mesopotamia, Sumer, the land between two rivers, the Tigris and the Euphrates.

By 486 BCE, Persians, Indo-Europeans, also called Aryans, would control all of Mesopotamia and, in fact, all of that part of the world from the Northeast of Greece, to Egypt, from Palestine and the Arabian Peninsula across Mesopotamia and all the way to India and they did it through the religious-based eschatological concept of manifest destiny.[22] The governors of these newly developed countries conquered Sumer and infused their languages, cultural habits and belief systems with the people of the land. The Achaemenid, Seleucid and Sassanid empires invaded, successively occupied the land and ruled over this region. Invaders continued to transgress past the borders of their own spheres of influence to amass more land, enrich their empires and increase their wealth from the natural resources of a land rich with gold, diamonds, and oil. Eventually there was an Islamic Conquest of Persia by Arabs and Persia is now known as Iran [Aryan].

---

22 http://wsu.edu:8080/~dee/MESO/PERSIANS

To escape the displacement and onslaught of invasions, the people of the land, migrated north, south, east and west to more peaceful environments. People of color migrated and inhabited lands now known as Europe. In ancient times, people called themselves by the names of the cities that they constructed and inhabited or for events that happened there. Romulus, is the name of the African albino who founded Rome, and the eponym from which Rome was named.[23]   After the destruction of Jerusalem and the massacre of black human beings by the Romans in 70 CE, there was a Roman domination of the land between the Tigris and the Euphrates. Wars with Rome compelled hundreds of thousands to escape to North Africa where there was a large Hebrew population. Hebrews migrated over 1400 years to the West where cities were established and businesses prospered. The first major Israelite empire of central Africa was that of Ghana. For nearly a thousand years, from approximately 300 CE, until late in the 13th century, when the Kingdom of Mali assumed dominance, Ghana, the Gold Kingdom, was dominant in the tropics of Africa.[24]

Black Hebrews fled religious persecution and religious domination by the Persians, forced conversion to Islam or death by the Arabs who eventually conquered the Persians and forced baptism to Catholicism and a triune god by the Romans.

Enslaved Africans represented many different peoples, each with distinct cultures, religions, and languages. Most originated from the coast or the interior of West Africa, between today's Senegal and Angola. Other slaves originally came from Madagascar and Tanzania in East Africa.[25]

---

23 Most people consider this a myth but see Alexander Calder's *Romulus and Remus,* a wire sculpture memorializing this event and Frances Cress Welsing, *The Isis (Yssis) Papers* for further indicators on this subject.

24 http://www.hebrewisraelites.org/Exile.htm

25 National Park Service, U.S. Department of the Interior, Report 2000.

Slavery

The "scattering," deportation, displacement, and forced enslavement of Black Hebrew people is referred to as the "diaspora." The 300 million estimated deaths that resulted from this experience is known as "the Real-Holocaust."[26]   The Real-Holocaust is described as "the great or massive destruction of life, both physical and mental, of people of African descent," black people.[27]   The Arab-Slave Trade began as early as 200 CE. Hebrews were taken from mainland East Africa and sold in markets in the Arabian Peninsula and the Persian Gulf. Eventually, they were transported via the Indian Ocean to other parts of the world. The Atlantic-Slave Trade began much later around 1440 CE and people were then channeled to the Americas through what was known as the Middle Passage. Many did not survive.

"Supplying both the Indian Ocean and Atlantic Ocean markets, Arab slavers, like their European counterparts, could be very ruthless, with eyewitnesses having observed them, on one occasion, cut the throats of two hundred forty slaves and throw them overboard when their "dhow" or small ship was being chased by a paddle-wheel frigate. Arab slavers also were notorious for the "manufacture of eunuchs" – cutting the genital organs from enslaved boys and selling them cheaply, with only one child in twenty surviving the operation. Incredible barbarism!"[28]

This trading in humans was dominated throughout the fifteenth and sixteenth centuries by the Iberian nations of Portugal and Spain, and continued throughout the seventeenth century by the British and their American counterparts. European nations fought one another for the privilege of managing this trade.[29]   Portugal, which ran the first leg, was ousted by Holland which in turn surrendered supremacy on the African coast to France and England. Trading arrangements

---

26 Gyasi A. Foluke, *The Real Holocaust,* Carlton Press Corp. 1995, NY. p. 9.
27 *Id.*
28 *Id.* p. 64.
29 Lerone Bennett Jr., *Before the Mayflower, A History of Black America,* 8th ed. Johnson Publishing Co., Inc., USA, May 2007, p. 46.

existed between Europeans – French, Swedish, Danish, Portuguese, Dutch, English and Prussian traders to process Africans bought and stolen.[30]

"We are all in the same boat."

"Now that the whole ship's cargo were confined together, it became absolutely pestilential. The closeness of the place, and the heat of the climate ... almost suffocated us ... The shrieks of the women, and the groans of the dying rendered it a scene of horror almost inconceivable ... I began to hope that death would soon put an end to my miseries."

Olaudah Equiano, sold from Africa into
New World slavery at age 12.[31]

Black Africans were put ashore from a ship at Jamestown, Virginia in the year 1619, only a decade after the founding of England's first successful colony in the Americas.[32] In the eighteenth century, thousands of captured Africans were held in Sierra Leone, West Africa to be boarded on ships bound for South Carolina and Georgia.[33] Their descendants are known as the Gullah and they are represented throughout the Sea Islands, the Bahamas, Oklahoma, Texas and Mexico. In the nineteenth and twentieth centuries the slave trade continued even after the abolition of slavery in the United States in 1865. As Africans were taken out of Africa, the European "scramble" for Africa began. Around the last quarter of the nineteenth century (1870-1900) the Europeans, generally the Dutch, Portuguese, British, Spanish, French, Italians and Germans held a series of conferences, at Brussels in 1876 and Berlin in 1884-85, to geographically partition Africa into "spheres of influence"

---

30 *Id.*
31 National Park Service, U.S. Department of the Interior, Report 2000.
32 James Mellon, *Bullwhip Days, The Slaves Remember, an Oral History*, Introduction, Avon Books Trade Printing, New York 1984 p. xi.
33 Wilbur Cross, *Gullah Culture in America*, Praeger Publishers, Westport, CT 2008 p. viii.

among themselves, without, of course, consulting Africans and irrespective of existing African territorial boundaries – imperialism and arrogance *par excellence*![34]

Kum Ba Yah, My Lord, Kum Ba Yah
Kum Ba Yah, My Lord, Kum Ba Yah
Kum Ba Yah, My Lord, Kum Ba Yah
Oh Lord, Kum Ba Yah

Selected Lyrics, A Slave Song of African-American Origin
Translation: Come Here Yah, from Gullah creole spoken by
slaves on the Sea Islands of Georgia and North Carolina

The capture of lands and the enslavement of people was accomplished by lies, deceit, fear tactics, force, maiming, death threats, murder, lynching, the use of weapons of mass destruction,[35] rape, mentacide and genocide. The narratives of enslaved black people published in <u>Bullwhip Days</u>, and excerpted here tell only part of the story.

> … When ships would land in Africa, de black folks would go down to watch dem, and sometimes dey would show dem beads and purty things dey carried on de ship. One day, when my daddy and his brother, Peter, wuz standing round looking, de boss-man axed dem if dey wanted to work and handed dem a package to carry on de boat. When dey got dere, dey see so many curious things dey jest wander around' looking, and before dey know it de boat has pulled off from de landing and dey is way out in de water and kain't he'p themselves. So dey jest brought 'em on over to Georgy and sold 'em. Dere wuz a boat load of 'em, all stolen. Dey sold my daddy and uncle, Peter, to Mr. Holland. Dey wuz put on a block and Mr.

---

34 Gyasi A. Foluke, *The Real Holocaust*, Carlton Press Corp., New York 1995, p. 73.

35 *Id.* p. 74.

Holland buyed 'em. Dat wuz in Dalton, Georgy.... - *Chaney Mack, p.49*

Ole Missus and young Missus told the little slave children that the stork brought the white babies to their mothers, but that the slave children were all hatched out from buzzard's eggs. And we believed it was true. - *Katie Sutton, p. 39*

Ise 'membah one slave dat gits whupped so bad hims neber gits up. Hims died. We-uns chillluns would go roun' what hims was an' look at 'im. De marster lets we-uns do dat, Ise guess, fo' to larn we-uns dat 'tis best' fo' to min'. - *Teshan Young, p. 41*

...We served our mistress and master, in slavery time, and not God. - S*arah Douglas, p. 185*

...It was a raw cowhide strap, 'bout two feet long, and she started to pourin' it on me all de way upstairs. I didn't know what she was whipin' me 'bout, but she pour it one, and she pour it on. Turrectly she say, "You can't say 'Marse Henry,' Miss? You can't say 'Marse Henry'?"

"Yes'm! Yes'm! I kin say 'Marse Henry'!"

Marse Henry was just a little boy 'bout three or four years old – come 'bout half way up to me. She wanted me to say "Massa" to him – a baby! - *Rebecca Grant, p. 41*

Marster preach to de white folks Sunday mo'nin'. Den, at night, all de masters roun' dat country sen' dey slaves, an' he preach to us. He had two fav'rit tex'es he uster preach from to de slaves. One was, "Serv'nts, obey your marsters." ... De other tex' was, "Thou shalt not steal." He preach dat over an' over, to de niggers. Dey couldn' read deir Bibles, so dey hatter b'liebe jis' what he say.

Since I's got to readin' an'studyin', I see some of de chu'ches is wrong, an' de preachers don' preach jis like de Bible say. - *Jack White, p. 197*

Lordy, mist'ess, ai't nobody never told you it was agin'de law larn a nigger to read and write, in slavery time? White folks would chop your hands off for dat quicker dan dey would for 'most anything else. Dat's jus' a say', "Chop your hands off."... - *William McWhorter, p. 197*

When Dr. Cannon found out dat his carriage driver had larned to read and write whilst he was takin' de doctor's chillum to and f'om school, he had dat nigger's thumbs cut off, and put another boy to doin' de drivin' in his place. – *Tom Hawkins p. 198*

My mother, she didn't work in the field. She worked at a loom. She worked so long and so often that once she went to sleep at the loom. Her master's boy saw her and told his mother. His mother told him to take a whip and wear her out. He took a stick and went out to beat her awake. He beat my mother till she woke up. When she woke up, she took a pole out of the loom and beat him nearly to death with it. He hollered, "Don't beat me no more, and I won't let 'em whip you." She said, "I'm goin' to kill you. These black titties sucked you, and then you come out here to beat me." And when she left him, he wasn't able to walk.

And that was the last I seen of her until after Freedom. She went out and got an old cow that she used to milk - Dolly, she called it. She rode away from the plantation, because she knew they would kill her, if she stayed. - *Ellen Cragin, p. 238*

...but one thing I do know was that white men got plenty chilluns by the nigger women. They didn't ask them. They just took them. I heard plenty 'bout that. Rosa will tell you the same. - *Jack and Rosa Maddox, p. 121*

I 'member once when I tole 'bout seein' a nigger runnin' away, boss got his hymn book, set down, put me 'cross his knees, an' as he'd sing de hymns, he'd whup me to de tune of 'em. Believe me, when he got through, I didn' set down for a week, an' I ain' never seed no more niggers runnin' away, neither! - *Anderson Williams, p. 299*

A Yankee...said, "Nigger, the government is going to give every ex-slave forty acres of land and a mule, but it will cost twenty dollars to make out the papers. Meet me here with twenty dollars next Monday morning, and I'll make over forty acres of this fine land to you, and give you the mule later."

Well, my father got up the twenty dollars and met the man and gave it to him, and received a paper from him. But father couldn't read.... He took his deed to a local white man to read. And this is the wording of that Yankee's deed: "This is to certify that this Negro has been able to secure a piece of paper called a deed to forty acres and a mule, and I hope that he gets both, someday." Of course, my daddy never forgave that Yankee for cheating him. - *The Reverend W. B. Allen, p. 342*

I never knowed 'bout no slave uprisin's. They'd had to uprose wid rocks an' red clods. The black man couldn't shoot. He had no guns. The slaves had so much work they didn't know how to have a uprisin'. The better you be to your master, the better he treat you. The white preachers teach that in the church.- *Cal Woods, p. 241*

A Slave is a human being. A Slave is a worker.

Working from sun-up to sun-down, a slaves' work was never done. Guyana, 'the land of many waters,' and the land where I was born, was built by the labors of African slaves. The tasks of the enslaved, among others, were to erect the living quarters, construct the sea wall, build dams, drainage canals and irrigation ditches, graze the land for cattle, cultivate the soil and cut cane to supply the European market with sugar. Further, to show the amount of human labor involved, a "100 million tons of earth had to be moved to create the plantations along the coast." The Venn Commission found that "each square mile of arable land needs on an average some 49 miles of drainage canals and 16 miles of high level irrigation canals if it has to be worked."[36]

The Portuguese established political dominance in Brazil which sent its tobacco, sugar, manioc, beans, spirits, cloth and sweetmeats eastward in exchange for the slaves and to a lesser extent, palm oil, rice, ivory, gold and the products of Asia.[37] In Brazil, slaves were branded Catholic.

Professor Marco Polo Hernandez Cuevas devotes his academic career to studying the African presence in Mexico. His work is part of a larger research tradition that studies the displacement of Africans by Europeans throughout the world.[38] Professor Hernandez cites expert estimates of as many as 11 million African slaves being brought to the Americas between 1450 and 1900. During this period, he says, about 2.5 million of these African slaves were taken into the Spanish Empire, about 4 million were taken to Brazil and about 500,000 were taken to North America. According to Hernandez, as many as 300,000 Africans were taken to Mexico. Hernandez said that he is committed to teaching students about the traditions and experience of African Mexicans.

There is an African presence all over this planet. The libraries are full of books on black history and slavery if anyone reading this wants to look further on any of these topics. I mention Guyana above because I am personally linked to Guyana. I was born there when it was British Guiana. My birth certificate says my parents are natives. I am personally linked to the Portuguese. The Portuguese were one of the first to enslave Africans. My great-grandmother was Portuguese and when her husband died, she and my great-grandfather, a black man who was born in Barbados, and whose first name I do not even know, married and managed a coal shop in Guyana. [When I asked my Uncle Eric, who is now in his nineties, what my great-grandmother's name was, he said her name was Avo, which means

---

36 Peter Simms, *Trouble in Guyana*, Allen & Unwin, Ltd., London, 1966, p. 35.

37 E. Bradford Burns, *A History of Brazil*, 3rd edition, Columbia University Press, NY 1993, p. 42.

38 http://web.nccu.edu/campus/echo/c-marco.html

grandmother in Portuguese and that his grand-father's last name was Greaves.]

Guyana was initially colonized by the British, (British Guiana) and other parts of Guyana were colonized by the Dutch and the French. I mention the Portuguese for another reason, to show how the Portuguese and their collaborations with the Spanish influenced much of the life and language here in North and South America. The Spanish conquered land and imposed their language and culture on the people of the land. I mention Mexico to show the African presence in Mexico through the Hebrew-Phoenicians who migrated to the Americas, and the Maya who inhabited lands in Mexico, as well as Guatemala, and Peru.

"Why?"

"Manifest Destiny" spiritually, socially and philosophically fueled the wars, transgressions and enslavement of black people. Slavers were consumed by greed to monopolize and colonize the world and used religion to justify their actions and although as you see here, black people were spiritually connected to the life-force of creation, the slavers said they were "heathens" and it was their duty to "save" them. The concept of "manifest destiny" was promoted with total disregard for human beings, under the pretense that the enslaved were animals, beasts of burden, who were supposed to serve whites and to fulfill their ideologies.

The following statements, by some of the most influential figures in European and American history, constitute the mindsets which supported the institution of slavery.

> I am apt to suspect the Negroes to be naturally inferior to the whites. There scarcely ever was a civilized nation of that complexion, nor even an individual, eminent either in action or speculation. - *David Hume, philosopher: Essays, Morals, and Political, 1742*

Those creatures are all over black and with a flat nose can scarcely be pitied. It is hardly to be believed that God, who is a wise Being, should place a soul, especially a good soul, in such a black, ugly body. It is so natural to look upon color as the criterion of human nature... - *Baron de Montesquieu, philosopher: Spirit of Laws, 1748*

Why increase the sons of Africa, by planting them in America, where we have so fair an opportunity, by excluding all blacks and tawnys, of increasing the lovely white and red? - *Benjamin Franklin: Observations Concerning the Increase of Mankind, 1753*

It is now entirely clear to me that, as his cranial structure and hair type prove, Lassalle is descended from the Negroes who joined Moses' flight from Egypt (that is assuming his mother, or his paternal grandmother, did not cross with a nigger). Now this union of Jewry and Germanism with the negro-like basic substance must necessarily result in a remarkable product. The officiousness of the fellow is also nigger-like. - *Karl Marx: Letter to Friedrich Engels, 1862*

The round eyes of the Negroes, their flat noses, thick lips, ears of different shape, the wool on their heads, the measure of their intelligence, place between them and the other species prodigious differences. - *Voltaire, author-philosopher: Essai sur les Mouers, 1829*

I have no purpose to introduce political and social equality between the white and the black races. There is a physical difference between the two, which, in my judgement, will probably forever forbid their living together upon the footing of perfect equality; and inasmuch as it becomes a necessity that there must be a difference, I am in favor of the race to which I belong having the superior position. - *Abraham Lincoln, U.S. President: Debate with Stephen Douglas, 1858*

The old antislavery school says that women must stand back, that they must wait until male Negroes are voters. But we say, if you will not give the whole loaf of justice to an entire, give it to the most intelligent first. If intelligence, justice, and morality are to be placed in the government, then let the question of (white) woman be brought up first and that of the Negro last. - *Susan B. Anthony, Reply to Frederick Douglass, 1869*

> Take up the White Man's Burden
> Send forth the best ye breed
> Go bind your sons to exile
> To serve your captive's need
> To wait in heavy harness
> On fluttered folk and wild
> Your new-caught, sullen peoples,
> Half devil and half child.

> *Rudyard Kipling, author-poet:*
> *"The White Man's Burden," 1899*

...it was true in a certain sense that all men of a particular nation were created equal, but not that a man in Central Africa was created equal to a European. - *Lord Balfour, Prime Minister of Great Britain: Opinion expressed at the Paris Peace Conference, 1919*

We shall encounter an Africanized America in which the white race by the inexorable law of numbers will end by being suffocated by the fertile grandsons of Uncle Tom ... Are we to see within a century a Negro in the White House? - *Benito Mussolini, dictator of Italy: Statement warning white Americans against miscegenation, 1934*

...(I) loathed their black hides, their filthy persons, and their odiferous aroma! ... to me it is a mystery how there can be any yellow faces among them. I don't see how any Southern gentleman could have been guilty. - *Ambrose Bierce, author: To his friend Walter Neal*

How far the gentlemen of dark complexion will get with their independence, now that they have declared it, I don't know. There are very serious difficulties in their way. The vast majority of the people of their race are but two or three inches removed from gorillas: it will be a sheer impossibility, for a long, long while, to interest them in anything above pork chops and bootleg gin. - *H. L. Mencken, critic: Excerpt from his review of The New Negro in "American Mercury," February, 1926*

Stephen, if it weren't for you wretched Britishers, we wouldn't have any Negroes in this country anyway; we wouldn't have this mess! - *Billy Graham, evangelist: To Stephen Olford, 1940*

Nature has colour-coded groups of individuals so that statistically reliable predictions of their adaptability to intellectually rewarding and effective lives can easily be made and profitably be used by the pragmatic man in the street. - *William B. Shockley, Stanford University Professor and Nobel Prize winner in Physics, 1972*

In the United States, "manifest destiny" held that territorial expansion was not only inevitable but divinely ordained. This doctrine was used to support the annexation of Texas and later used by expansionists in all political parties to justify the acquisition of California, the Oregon Territory, and Alaska. By the end of the 19th century, "manifest destiny" was being applied to the proposed annexation of various islands in the Caribbean Sea and the Pacific Ocean, "from sea to shining sea."[39] This idea was also behind American political actions overseas through the spread of "democracy" throughout the world and this concept clearly played a role in twentieth century American foreign policy.[40]

The Last Frontier

Hebrews, black people, are now thought to be the real discoverers of America. They were here before Columbus. The Hebrew-

---

39 http://encarta.msn.com/encyclopedia_761568247/Manifest_Destiny. html

40 http://www.wisegeek.com/what-is-manifest-destiny.htm

Phoenicians navigated their way across the globe and planted their roots throughout the diaspora. Present day Hebrews such as the LawKeepers, are a definitive source of Hebrew doctrine. This organization of Hebrew Yisraelites, (not Jewish) Israelites of so-called African Descent (Black) scattered throughout the diaspora, define their primary purpose is:

"To exalt, honor and give praise and glory to the Holy ONE of Yisrael YHWH; Do the Laws given to Moses to give to the children of Israel; and return to the land of our forefathers, the land of Yisrael. Also to assist and act as an advocate for likeminded Hebrew Yisraelites who have returned to their heritage, and who desire to return to their homeland, the land of our forefathers, the land of Yisrael."

"We do not embrace the Greek writings also known as the New Testament nor its teachings of human sacrifice or a triune godhead, and do not embrace JC/Yeshua as our saviour following the admonition found in Exodus 6:3 "Thou shalt have no other gods before me" and Isaiah 43:11 "I even I, am YHWH and beside me there is no savior." We are here to herald forth the truth concerning our GOD YHWH and his "peculiar people" who have been scattered in the lands of their captivity as of this day, specifically to the nation of Yisrael in the "Valley of Dry Bones" who have lost their identity as a nation."

The LawKeepers

"Who Am I?"

*They have said, come and let us cut them off
from being a nation that the name of Israel
may be no more in their remembrance.*[41]

To know is the difference.

A Survivor

I am an individual. I am who I am, a hueman[42] being. I am one of a people whose life has been disrupted by forces beyond my control and I have survived in spite of the dehumanizing institution of slavery, loss of memory and identity. I am still here.

I found myself and when I found myself, I found my God and I believe my God is life Itself. I am part of humanity, a living, breathing, natural hueman being. I believe my God is the Universal Intelligence and that I am part of the universe. I believe my God is the World and the Word in It. I believe my God is my conscience. I believe my God is in me. I call my God Yahuwah, Whoever Yah be. My God is no mystery to me. I have the right to believe what I want to believe and to be who I want to be and no one should take those rights from me.

---

41 *Id*. Windsor, n. 1 p. 123.

42 Frances Cress Welsing, *The Isis (Yssis)* Papers, Third World Press, Chicago: Illinois, 1992.

Conclusions

"War is not the answer for only love can conquer hate."

Marvin Gaye, singer, from recording,
"What's Going On"

"It is all love – always has been."

Carlton B. Ingleton, Artist, 1940-2007

This was not meant to be a history lesson. It is not a comprehensive historical review. It is impossible for me to document over 8,000 years of history in these pages. This is a very personal search. I started my search with one word, 'bubbie' and this is what I found. The data was selected to enlighten my journey in search of links to my existence and I found them.

I am linked to a life-force, the God of the Universe who I like to call Yah and whether one chooses to believe the creation story or not, it is the only story I have. I am linked to all my ancestors, kings, queens and slaves and my ancestors were originally, people of color, out of the land, between the Tigris and the Euphrates, Sumer, Ethiopia, Africa, in the East. I am linked to Asia, South America, the Maya, and the Gullah who I identify with based on my color and culture. This is part of my tradition that was found and confirmed in my search.

I found the visible link to my existence is my color. If it were not for my color, I would not have a clue to my ancestry or my culture and I would not have a story. No one is God and no one knows the nature of God. All we know is what we see and what is manifested in life and I choose to call what is known and unknown, seen and unseen, God, Yah, and I have a right to my own belief. I believe in the original Hebrew doctrine and I identify with all Hebrews who share this belief. I believe in the concept of African spirituality and I believe in life and what is real. I found that I am responsible for my own being and that no one has the right to captivate my mind or own my body.

Slavery is wrong! It is wrong to enslave someone, to force someone to adopt your religious thought, to brand someone to possess his or her mind and body, to brand someone to believe what you believe and to kill someone because they do not look like you. Every one has the right to his or her own destiny. It is not right to hate someone because they have color. I am a person, a hueman being. I have my own mind in my own body.

Love is the answer! I love myself! I love my people! I love everyone! I found that we are all related and whether we came to the Americas by force or free will, as a Nation, we are all connected to the people who came before us and we are all connected to our land. This is our world!

Finding Self

"I believe this world has always been here. This world has no beginning. It has no end. It has developed in space and time. It has always existed and this is The Way It is."

I am who I am, a human (hueman) being, a woman of color, a Black woman. When we come into this world, we come with a body and mind that has already been made up. We did not create the world; we did not create ourselves. This has been done already. Who created the world and who created us? We say God created the world and God created us because that is what we believe and we believe this because it is already in our minds. God already put it there. How do I know that? I don't know. I believe that and that belief is in my mind already. That is why I believe that the God in my mind is the universal intelligence because I think that this higher power, this higher force, this life force is Who made me up and Who made up my mind because I didn't make myself and I didn't make the world and I know no other man made the world because man is human. Man is not what we call God.

When I came into the world, I was born with color. I know that because I have color now. All we have when we come into this world are our bodies, our minds and our color. Some people do not have color. Color is the quintessential element that makes us Who, (sounds a little like Hue to me) we are. Color is a good thing. Dr. Frances Cress Welsing wrote *The Isis Papers* and in that book she talks about how good color is and you can read her if you like to know more about that. I just want to look at myself and other people like myself who have color because color makes us Who we are and when other people see us, that is what they perceive. When I look at myself, I see a person of color and when I see other people of color, I identify with them because we look alike. I think God made us with color because God wanted us to have color so we would be able to recognize each other as Who we are, human, hueman beings made by God with color. I identify with all people as living beings. I identify with all people of color who share similar experiences and have a common culture. We did not have to have color. Some people do not have color and I think I said that already but I may be trying to make a point and I think I did.

I think that if we recognize the color in us, we should recognize that God, put that color there and this is the way It is. I don't think God could have put that color there if God did not have color. That is why I call My God, Yahuwah. Why? Yahuwah to me means Ya (A, One God), hu (Who, hu, or hue) wah (A, An, Ah or Is). *A* means One. "An" also means One and was the name of a 'primary' God of Sumer, a place where civilized people lived thousands of years ago. These people called themselves *sag-gi-ga*, "the black-headed people" and their women wore their locks on the top of their heads. This suggests to me that these civilized people, based on their language, cultural practices, arts, architecture and astronomical discoveries were people of color, Black people who lived in a place, Sumer [people of Summer], known as the Garden of Eden, Ethiopiyah, Cush, also known as Mesopotamiyah, Babyloniyah (Babylon sounds like babyland, or birthplace to me, and babble sounds like baby-talk) and that this place, a fertile land between the Tigris and Euphrates Rivers, is the cradle of civilization, the birthplace of people of color, Black people.

You may say that I did not spell Ethiopiyah, Mesopotamiyah or Babyloniyah correctly and I may say that maybe Ethiopia, Mesopotamia and Babylonia were spelled differently and that in these instances, no matter how you spell it, you hear the sound of Yah, A, Ah, and I am just trying to make a point. This Yah word also sounds like Yes, or Yeah. It sounds right to me. However, I am not finished; bear with me. I am saying that just like we come here with bodies, and minds and color all made up, we come here with sounds that have already been made up. How do I know that? We talk, we cry and we didn't put those sounds in our mouths and I can say that I believe that God, Yah, put those sounds there because the sounds are there already (all ready). Spanish-speaking people have a word for done, finished, (in other words, already). Do you know what that word is? That word is Ya and it looks like and sounds like Yah to me.

Let me go on. The Accadians, and this is also spelled Akkadians, and could very well be spelled, Akkadiyahns, also lived in this same area, and they had a God of Wisdom they called EA. Say E and AH and what do you hear? Do you hear the Yah there? I do. The spelling has been changed but the sound remains the same. That is really saying something. That says to me that regardless of how many gods people had, as far back as we know, they had a belief in A, One God, Who Is. From where I stand now, I believe that what people called gods, (the earth, the sun, the sky) were attributes of God or that is what I believe – One God with many attributes – An Everything God, A God Who Is God, A God Who Is, A God Who Exists, and a God Who Is Manifested in hueman beings. I feel like I am from God and I think all human beings are from God. My grandmother, Angela Callender, always told me that my name, Anne was a God-blessed name and I know why? I think it is because my name Anne sounds very much like An, and the spelling is similar. I also see An and Angel in my grandmother's name and I think there are human beings who are real angels, good people. And, of course, I see 'a' and 'an' in every man and woman. I am just trying to make connections. I am trying to make sense of my world and the words in it and this is what I have come up with.

I understand some people say Jehovah and if you look closely, you will see a relationship between the two words, Je(Ya) ho(hu) vah(wah). I think Jehovah is a modern spelling of Yahuwah as much as Jah is a modern spelling of Yah. [Most recently I heard that there is no 'J' in Hebrew.] So there! I am making connections. That is all. It took me a long time to even say Yah or Yahuwah. Why? Because this word was taken out of our mouths when we were taken away from our land, Ethiopiyah, and replaced with other words such as Arabic, Portuguese, Spanish, English, and French in our land. Our word was taken away! Our language was taken away! Our God was taken away!

From what I see and hear, A, An, Ya, Yah, Ea, Eah, sound alike to me and all mean the same thing, One God. I call my God, Yah, because It makes sense to me. I do not believe that we have a Sumeriyan God or an Accadian God, or a Catholic God, or a Jewish

God, or an Israelite God or a Muslim God or an Egyptian God. God has put God's name in place and time so that we don't forget Who our God is. I believe I have experienced God by connecting with the God within; I believe God put God's self in ourselves, in our world, the earth, the sky, the rivers, the universe and I think I know a little about Who God is but how would I really know Who God is. I am not God so I have to say Whoever God Is because I don't know everything. We are kind of limited like that; we are only human. We can only imagine what God is like. I like to think that:

God has a name. I didn't make this up. You didn't make this up. It is here already, Yah. God is the God Who Is. This God exists as a life-force. We come into being in a world that is already here, already made up. We did not create the world. If you don't believe what I believe, search yourself (Ya'self). Recognize the Yah in You. It is there. Just as I can see the Y in You, I know you can see It too.

My God is Life Itself.

My God is the Universal Intelligence.
We did not create our mind. We come into a world that is here already. Ya. Yah.

My God is the World and the Word in It.
I know you see the word in world; Bible – 'bi' means two; 'ble, Babel and babble' have something to do with words, or talking enthusiastically or excessively. You can say that the Bible is two words. You know that if you believe in God, there is only, One way, Yahway, Yahwey, and one Word, the right way.

My God is my Conscience.
Con means 'with' in Spanish, e.g. conmigo (with me); contigo (with you); 'con' has a lot of meanings in English but the one I would use in this context is the original meaning for 'con' which is, to know, learn, study, to commit to memory; to study or examine closely. You know what your "conscience" is. You see the 'science' in there. I could say that your conscience is the science inside your mind, what you know, and what you are able to reflect on. I have always said that

babies come here with brains. I can say our minds have already been made up and our understanding, our conscience, is in there.

<u>My God is in me.</u>
God is in my mind.

<u>I call my God Yahuwah, Whoever Yah be.</u>
We know some things about God or what we would like to believe, but then we don't know everything. God is Whoever God Is.

<u>My God is no mystery to me.</u>
My God is no mystery (misstory) and I don't have to go there. We all know that what we have been told about God may not be true because Who really knows and mysteries (misstories) about God have been made up.

This is what I believe and my beliefs are based on my faith and my relationship with my God. You can believe whatever you want to about God. My beliefs work for me.

Inspirations

Celebrate You!

Think for Ya'self!

Do not believe everything you read, see or hear.

Know yourself!

Be yourself!

Love yourself!

Think before you talk; think before you act.

This is your life; do the best you can!

S.O.O.S. Stay Out Of Space

MYOB Mind Your Own Business

UBU

War is uncivilized, barbaric and wrong!

Forgive; Never Forget

Give Thanks!

Words My Husband Passed On To Me

(Author Anonymous)

The most worthless emotion – SELF-PITY
The most beautiful attire – SMILE
The most prized possession – INTEGRITY
The most powerful channel of communication – PRAYER
The most important thing in life – GOD
The most destructive habit – WORRY
The greatest joy – GIVING
The greatest loss – LOSS OF SELF-RESPECT
The most satisfying works – HELPING OTHERS
The ugliest personality trait – SELFISHNESS
Our greatest natural resource – OUR YOUTH
The greatest motivator – ENCOURAGEMENT
The greatest problem to overcome – FEAR
The most effective sleeping pill – PEACE OF MIND
The most crippling failure disease – EXCUSES
The most powerful force in life – LOVE
The most dangerous pariah – A GOSSIPER
The world's most incredible computer – THE BRAIN
The worst thing to be without – HOPE
The deadliest weapon – THE TONGUE
The two most power-filled words – I CAN

The Ten Commandments

1. I am The Lord your God, Who brought you out of the land of Egypt, out of the house of bondage. You shall have no other gods before Me. [One God]

2. You shall not make for yourself a graven image, or any likeness of anything that is in heaven above, or that is in the earth beneath, or that is in the water under the earth; you shall not bow down to them or serve them; for I The Lord your God am a jealous God, visiting the iniquity of the fathers upon the children to the third and the fourth generation of those who hate Me, but showing steadfast love to those who love Me and keep My Commandments. [One God.]

3. You shall not take The Name of the Lord your God in vain; for the Lord will not hold him guiltless who takes His Name in vain. [Do not say God's name in vein with any other name. Do not call my name if I am not your God.]

4. Remember the Sabbath day, to keep it holy. Six days you shall labor, and do all your work; but the seventh day is a Sabbath to The Lord your God; in it you shall not do any work, you, or your son, or your daughter, your manservant, or your maidservant, or your cattle, or the sojourner who is within your gates.

5. Honor your father and your mother, that your days may be long in the land which The Lord your God gives you. [I believe that mothers and fathers should also honor their children.]

6. You shall not kill.

7. You shall not commit adultery.

8. You shall not steal.

9. You shall not bear false witness against your neighbor. [Don't lie.]

10. You shall not covet [desire] your neighbor's house; you shall not covet [desire] your neighbor's wife, or his manservant, or his maidservant, or his ox, or his ass, or anything that is your neighbor's.

Moses (Exodus 20:2-17 RSV)

NGUZO SABA: THE SEVEN PRINCIPLES

(N-GOO-ZOE-SAH-BAH)

UMOYA (OO-MOE-YAH) - UNITY

KUJICHAGULIA (COO-GEE-CHA-GOO-LEE-AH) – SELF-DETERMINATION

UJIMA (OO-GEE-MA) – COLLECTIVE WORK AND RESPONSIBILITY

UJAMAA (OO-JAH-MAH) – COOPERATIVE ECONOMICS

NIA (NEE-AH) – PURPOSE

KUUMBA (KOO-M-BAH) – CREATIVITY

IMANI (E-MAH-NE) – FAITH

[These Ethiopian principles form the basis of Kwanzaa, introduced by Ron Karenga to uplift all Afrikin people]

Proverbs
(Words my mother passed on to me)

Do not take advantage of anyone and do not have anyone take advantage of you.

If you have your hand in the lion's mouth, take it out slowly.

Provocation leads to murder.

If you do something wrong, tell God you are sorry and don't do it again.

Black people story never done.

Cleanliness is next to Godliness.

Anything [anyone] can come clean.

Keep your hands to yourself.

Take your time.

There is an end to every rope.

Mouth open – story jump out.

Forgive and Forget.

Prescript
03/05/2006

I am. You are the descendants from the slaves in Africa, Egypt. We are the same people. We are Hebrew.

It's so simple.

You don't have to look any further. The slaves that came to America and the slaves who went to Israel are the same people.

I am having an experience today. I feel the truth in me. And I know it's real because tears came to my eyes on knowing and I started to shake.

God Is Real – Israel. God is It!

Forget about all the others! God is everything!

I am not shaking anymore. I feel strong. Let me go and find out about myself. Now I know what I have to do. Let's spread the Word.

You don't have to look in a history book. It is not going to be there. Look in your heart, your mind and it is so clear.

You don't have to read about it.

It is written in your soul.

God Is Real – Israel.

The same God who took us out of bondage, put us in bondage and is going to take us out of bondage again.

Let's get together! Be real – Israel.

Prescript
11/13/2006

Bush has to stop!
This is about the land!
God is (crossed out)
The Cre (crossed out)
Ja (crossed out)
Yah is in charge!

I am having the same feeling. I went back to bed and I had to get up
to write this down.

Yah is here!
The white man has to correct his ways.
If you think the WTC was bad ... If you think Katrina was bad ...

Yah is here to clean up the world.

I felt Yah in Brazil
I felt Yah in Kansas
I feel Yah here
I know what it feels like – lights.

The flag – I can't do the flag. The flag has to be made by someone. It looks like this.

Yah is here to claim the world.
It feels like energy, in my head, right across my eyes

Praise the Creator in the name of Yah! So everybody can understand. [Please, It's only three letters.]

We have to change or else some serious stuff is going to go down.

I have to get ready.
We have to get ready.

The Creator is not a man.
The Creator is the Creator.

(I'm seeing a lot of green.)
I must not be afraid.

Yah is going to be doing some stuff if Ya'll don't get it together.

How is Yah going to take the land?
Don't worry about it.

For Soledad and Obama
2008

To be Black in America is a dichotomy – one foot in Ya'land and the other out to sea.

To be Black in America is a promise of equality.

To be Black in America is to love the people who hate you, worship their gods, the people you pay rent to.

To be Black in America is to love yourself and each other, your families, your color and culture.

To be Black in America is to want to be, free to live, and die in peace.

"King Kong"

We are the Kong (Congo)

We are the agAPE you are looking for

We are your Mammys and your Daddys

Your Isis and your Ibro

We are your ancestors!

Reviews and Papers

"The Ten Commandments"

"The Ten Commandments" aired on WABC-7 on April 10th and April 11th and was not updated to reflect a black Moses. (Read about Moses in Rudolph R. Windsor, *From Babylon to Timbuktu, A History of the Ancient Black Races Including the Black Hebrews*, Exposition Press, Jericho, NY, 1973 pp. 23,24,34,36,66-70.) The producer, Robert Halmi Sr., and RHI Entertainment went out of their way to authenticate this version of "The Ten Commandments" casting actors from all over the globe – Argentina, France, Lebanon, Scotland, and Hungary – to name a few, but overlooked the color of the main character in this saga. When asked about the attention to historical accuracy, Robert Halmi Sr., stated that this "Ten Commandments" incorporated historical details discovered since Cecil B. DeMille's production was made. He insisted that this "Ten Commandments" was researched thoroughly, that the expertise of Christian and Jewish scholars was engaged and 20,000 extra actors appear in detailed costumes and religious paraphernalia reminiscent of the era. (www.rhifilms.com)

"The Ten Commandments" depicts the life of Moses, one of our most memorable Hebrew liberators. Moses, as a child, was raised by a black princess in Pharaoh's palace in Egypt, Africa. The Pharaoh was pure black. (Windsor p. 69) Hebrew slaves emerged in Egypt as the largest group of black people who were eventually led out of slavery by Moses into Israel. (Windsor p. 64) The story of Moses has roots in the land of Ethiopia. Ancient Ethiopia was one land and there were two Ethiopian nations, Ethiopia, in what is now known as Africa and Ethiopia, in what is now known as the Middle East. (Windsor pp. 14,21,22,26) At the end of the film, "the Promised Land" is referred to as "the land of milk and honey," Ethiopia.

The portrayal of people of color in "The Ten Commandments" is inaccurate. That RHI Entertainment visually dismisses people of color from the principal characterizations in this epic is a challenge to black identity and existence. The media continues, in the Cecil B. DeMille tradition, to "whitewash" images of ancient people of color while exploiting black cultural heritage. Why do historical programs insist on cutting people of color out of a legacy which came out of Africa, while negating our black images and disregarding our way of life? The story of Moses belongs to all of us and to visually misrepresent the central figures in this historical drama casts doubt on the content and undermines the scope of this presentation.

The intention to present, in Mr. Halmi's words, a "biblically accurate telling" of the Moses story was compromised in the casting. Moses was a black person and to neglect to visually attribute this quintessential element to his character is to make believe he did not really exist. RHI forges an identity of Moses that is intellectually misleading and psychologically damaging to all people who believe in God [Yahuwah] and the Ten Commandments. The actor, Dougray Scott, although an introspective, passionate and faithful Moses, did not render a true likeness. The motion picture making industry should consider the talents and knowledge within the 'Afrikin' community when depicting the black cultural experience. By doing so, they benefit the entire community by producing responsible and accurate image-making in their cultural programs.

Dulcie Ingleton
Brooklyn, NY
4/13/06

AN ANALYSIS OF *EVE'S BAYOU*

Starring

Samuel L. Jackson
Lynn Whitfield
Debbi Morgan
Jurnee Smollett
Meagan Good

Eve's Bayou, is an important work in African-American genre filmmaking that deals specifically with socio-psychological aspects of African-American culture, relating to the particular beliefs of the Batiste family who live on land near a Louisiana bayou. This Kasi Lemmons' film, situated amidst rich landscape, lush settings of flora, spacious skies and tranquil waters, represents an outstanding contribution to African-American cinema. The film exhibits visually compelling compositions and technical skills, dramatically rendering the lives of the Batistes, descendants of Eve, a slave woman and Jean Paul Batiste, the man she saved from cholera who, in return, gave her the land by the bayou and sixteen children, one of whom is named after her and is a central figure in the film. The soundtrack is filled with soulful songs by Erykah Badu, Bobby Blue Bland, Ray Charles, Etta James and musical innovations by the Utah Film Orchestra.

Eve's Bayou is strikingly realistic in appealing to one's sense of color and visual texture. Vibrant colors in red, purple and black and white characterize the authentic dress and dance costumes at soirees, and strolls across the bridge that lead to the market place. At the marketplace, the camera pans across luscious fruit, pineapples, strawberries, and brown potatoes lit by the sun, caressing each detail as it hovers over the colorful produce.

The richness of the Louisiana landscape is captured in the sprawling green lawns, beautifully sculptured homes, vastly distanced shots of wheat fields and the interplay of the sunlight and shadows on the bayou's tranquil waters. These settings are referred to intermittently throughout the film to focus one's attention to the serene and peaceful nature of this cinematic land. These images are designed to leave an impression of deep peace, beauty and serenity.

The rain scenes are textured with heavy downpours. Rain and thunderous sounds signify that something dramatic is happening. When Dr. Batiste and his wife, Roz, argue, the scene is accompanied by rain and thunder. Of the night that Cisely speaks to her sister Eve and accuses their father of kissing her inappropriately, sound effects of thunderous rain symbolize upheaval and discord. In Eve's dream sequence, rain and thunder signal the death of Harry, Mozelle's last husband.

The main characters in the film are very attractive and their beauty is complemented by physically constructed bodies and elegant costumes. The fine features and facial expressions of the film's main characters are shown in close-up shots of impeccable clarity and tonal hues. The smoothness of Roz's skin and the fluid nature of her pressed hair, is contrasted with the fibrous texture of the hair styles worn by Mozelle, her mother and her niece, Eve. Framed by a soft light, these close-up shots reveal the natural patterns and kinky beauty of untamed hair. Close-up shots focus not only on the characters in the film but are used to focus on their relationships of intimacy, friendship, and sisterly love when gossiping or sharing secrets. The camera closely catches an intimate moment with Mr. Mereaux's hands full of his wife, Matty, and her rear end at a house party in the home of Dr. Batiste with whom she is having an affair and later zooms toward Dr. Batiste and Matty in the shed with her legs dangling off the sides of his legs. The camera distances, however, to obscure the tragic drug use of Mozelle's client's son and the infidelity of her present lover's wife in one of her revelation sequences. The camera angles in to convey a sense of understanding or clarity and angles out to convey a sense of uncertainty, vagueness or improprieties.

The effects of brilliant lighting dominate the nature scenes, revelation sequences and illuminates the shimmering configurations on the waters of the bayou. Spots of light are integrated within the mise-en-scene in which Dr. Batiste hopefully counsels one of his recovering patients. Lights on the road clear the path for Dr. Batiste and his daughter Eve as she accompanies him on his patient visits. Overhead lights typify the bar scene. In a studio scene, an Etta James' *Sunday Kind of Love* soundtrack plays in the background and salon-styled paintings adorn the walls as Mozelle and her new lover, the artist Julian, bask in the light as it enters the studio. Lighting is a major indicator of dramatically drawing attention to a particular focal aspect of the mise-en-scene and symbolizes awareness, hope, direction and comfort.

The film is characterized by varying degrees of reality. In fact this leit motif is the recurring theme of the film and frames the essence of the film's meaning. It is through the relationships between real-life and dream/vision sequences that the meaning of the film is communicated. In essence, the theme in *Eve's Bayou* is that action and reaction is based on a selective choice of what one wants to believe to be real. This is supported by montage sequences based on the organization of mise-en-scene in which the viewer experiences both real and imaginary filmic situations and reinforces V. I. Pudovkin's formalist theory that the purpose of montage is to psychologically guide the viewer to support the film's narrative.

In the film, Eve possesses an intuitive sense and like her aunt, Mozelle, perceives in the realm of psychic vision. After awakening from a dream state Eve envisions the death of her aunt's husband, Harry. A coin that he actually gave her was spinning in the dream sequence. This coin connects her reality to the dream state in which what she envisions really does occur and confirms Eve's intuition. In this sequence the interaction between shots is the linkage that permits the meaning of the film to be communicated by providing support for a belief in transcendental vision. Parallel editing was recognized by V. I. Pudovkin in his analysis of the form and importance of the mise-en-scene in communicating meaning.

When Eve tells her sister Cisely that she saw her father and Mrs. Mereaux rubbing against each other in the shed, Cisely recreates the scene for Eve which is reenacted as a distance shot within the mise-en-scene, of what she wants Eve to believe and which, of course, was not related in any way to what she saw. And, because Eve believes Cisely's story that their father, Dr. Batiste, kissed her inappropriately, she makes assumptions about the father which causes her to solicit a market fortune teller to assist her in killing him. The father believes that his daughter, Cisely, kissed him passionately. In flashback, both versions of their actions in the mise-en-scene are equally believable. The father dies and although he was killed by Mr. Mereaux when Mr. Mereaux finds out that Dr. Batiste was having an affair with his wife, Eve believes she caused the death of her father with her psychic powers.

In one of the film's crucial sequences, where Mozelle, a psychic counselor, attends to her clients, montage plays a decisive role in guiding the psychological drama of the mise-en-scene by directing our thoughts to draw conclusions about the thematic intention of the film. It is structured narratively to reveal Mozelle's point of view by contrasting real-world and psychic phenomena. When Mozelle is about to advise her clients by foretelling, one is given a chance to examine the graphic power of the film media by participating in this filmic experience. The cinematographer uses deep focus to equalize the relationship between Mozelle and her client and to convince the viewer that both Mozelle and her client are equally contributing to the revelation. The color of the film changes to black and white and is followed by a speedy flashback of shadows and lights in the film and a flashback for Mozelle as she goes back into her mind to foretell an action. These actions are developed independently and simultaneously as well. Scenes in black and white are revealed to Mozelle which she then interprets for her clients. Both participants have their eyes closed and this symbolizes insight and a transference of inner visions. These are conventions used by the cinematographer to convey these parallel actions. It is apparent that the clear-cut montage sequences defy the lapses of passage from scene to scene and establish the cinematographic flow of the movements at a timely pace.

Voodoo is the medium through which Mozelle Batiste communicates with her clients, people who depend on her for psychic revelations, counseling and healing. When Mozelle reveals or interprets a situation of a client, the movement of psychic phenomena is presaged by shadows, flashbacks and shadowy patterns. This occurs in all of the vision and dream sequences. In another revelation sequence, a woman comes to Mozelle in search of her son. Mozelle extends her hands, palms up and the woman places her hand in Mozelle's, another signifier that something is about to occur. There is an immediate, now familiar, mise-en-scene that is cast in black and white with light and dark patterns, and shadows that signal a flashback. The imagery in this scene is distorted, out of focus and punctuated by abstract piano sounds. This imagery is unclear until Mozelle envisions and presents the client with the message.

In another revelation sequence, Mozelle reveals to Eve, her relationships with her three husbands who died. Although Mozelle, possesses superb psychic prowess, she cannot fully explain why these deaths occurred. She retraces for Eve the situation that caused her husband Maynard's death. A mirror is used as a convention of depth perception for Mozelle to engage Eve in a narrative on which to reflect these events. Mozelle enters the mirror and steps into the past and retells the story to Eve. Deep focus dominates the scene to make the viewer believe that the action is occurring in the same state of reality. This series of montage creates a mimesis of these states of reality which occur in the mise-en-scene.

The essence of what is communicated in this film is that our reality is what we believe. This is supported by the mise-en-scene in which we receive two versions of the inappropriate conduct between Dr. Batiste and his daughter as told by Cisely and Dr. Batiste. These two versions occur in a montage sequence with parallel points of view. Although each version is different, each version is believable. Mozelle foretells actions that are realized in the film sequences. For example, Mozelle "sees" that a car accident is going to occur which will involve a child. This causes Roz to protect her children from this accident by secluding them in the house for weeks. This passing of time in the house is symbolized by clocks ticking away, numbers increasing and references within the sequence to events occurring in the morning and at night. A child does meet with an accident and although the accident does not involve any of the Batiste children, Mozelle's mother reiterates that all of Mozelle's predictions come true. Their belief is grounded in manifestations of events that are predicted and realized within the passage of time. These manifestations confirm their belief in the supernatural and their trust in voodoo.

In retrospect, *Eve's Bayou* speaks to the human condition and the power of belief. This is substantiated by the leit motif used in the dream and vision sequences and the close proximity of real world and psychic phenomena which occur within the mise-en-scene. The theme of this film is that our visions, instincts, and perceptions are experiences which we selectively choose to incorporate in the scheme of living, acting and reacting to our world and we believe what we want to believe or believe what we make believable.

Fiction Into Film, *The Green Mile*

The Green Mile, Stephen King's serial novel about the prison environment and the execution of death row inmates is a tour-de-force in dramatic narrative. Although fiction, it deals realistically with real world issues such as race, racism, and injustice. The vestiges of the slave system are still evidenced in our social, educational, and economic systems. The psychological effects have surfaced in self-hate, worthlessness and depression. There is a crisis today surrounding legal services for poor people whose lives are at risk in the criminal courts, jails and prisons. The Equal Justice Initiative of Alabama reports racial bias and increased hostility to the plight of the disadvantaged exacerbates this crisis and undermines the equal administration of justice.

The book, *The Green Mile*, is written from the point of view of Paul Edgecombe, superintendent at Cold Mountain Penitentiary, who presides at the execution of death row inmates and centers on John Coffey and the circumstances surrounding his trial and wrongful conviction. Paul Edgecombe speaks of his relationship with John Coffey and the events which led to his execution for the rape and death of two white nine-year-old twin girls. He presents the stressful situation the inmates and prison guards are experiencing especially in John Coffey's case, since he is innocent. Paul Edgecombe's painful account of the events that occurred in 1932 is shrouded in mystery and magic and harshly reflects the presumptions of guilt and inequities of the criminal justice system.

The book relates in depth the experiences of other death row inmates. Eduard Delacroix was subjected to the torturous hands of the evil prison guard, Percy Wetmore, and suffered an electrically horrifying death. Beverly McCall put up with her husband's beatings but was not able to tolerate his affairs and spilled his guts on his two-tone shoes with his own razor when she found out he was cheating. Prez, escaped the death sentence 'because he was white,' and the stoic Indian, Arlen Bitterbuck, did not. Wild Bill Wharton, also known as Billy the Kid, was the one who raped and murdered the Detterick twins and he is on death row in Cold Mountain Penitentiary for a seemingly unrelated death. Stephen King brings these fictional characters to life and offers insight into, their motives, and their relationships with men, women and a mouse.

The film, *The Green Mile*, written and directed for the screen by Frank Darabont, visually situates one in the South. Fields of cotton dominate the Southern landscape. The novel does not offer much details about the land. The panoramic view is provided in the visual information on screen. Howling dogs signal the search party's efforts to find the bodies of the two dead girls. The camera surveys the area on the porch from where the two girls disappeared. Only a bloody red patch is left and bits of their nightgowns.

The camera spans the vastness of the exterior environment and then turns to the interior of the Cold Mountain Penitentiary where the lime-colored floor, flanked by prison cells, leads to the execution room. The electric chair, "Old Sparky," is an ever present fixture and the rain, thunder and lightning sequences that resound when someone walks the 'green mile' symbolizes the terrifying ordeal of death by electrocution.

The camera focuses on limping prisoners, preparations for death, walking the mile, prayer rehearsals, getting strapped and capped with the wet sponge and hooding the prisoner in black. The sounds of the heavy breathing, the humming of the electric chair, and the acts of the body shaking as the electricity passes through the body is an emotionally numbing experience for a viewer when the person is guilty. Imagine viewing this traumatic experience when the person about to be executed is innocent.

When John Coffey entered the Cold Mountain penitentiary, he was surrounded by a symbolically brilliant light. The low camera angles caused his image to dominate the screen and he appeared all the more powerful. He towered like a giant over the prison guards. To contain him and to restrict his movements, chains were strung across his chest and on his arms. Leg irons clasped his ankles connected by a large chain. The chains on his feet appeared minuscule in comparison to his ankles and feet.

The film, *The Green Mile*, is faithfully adapted from the novel and visually expresses the pain and psychological torture experienced by Paul Edgecombe. The role of Paul Edgecombe is performed by Tom Hanks. Tom, with beads of feverish sweat, shown by a night light, drops to his knees outside his house to urinate because he does not want his wife to hear his pain. Stephen King describes the pain Paul is hiding in the novel, as the throbbing of his groin, the hot, clogged and swollen feeling in his penis and the excruciating pain that accompanies the flow of urine like 'blood gushing from its tip.' John Coffey heals him of this persistent urinary infection and now Tom must play a part in John's death.

The mouse, also an inmate at the Cold Mountain Penitentiary, is a central character in the story and is contrasted with John Coffey physically and intellectually. The mouse, is small and intelligent because he is taught to perform tricks and rolls on a threadless spool. He is able to maneuver a piece of candy to his mouth with his tiny hands and he was even claimed to whisper in Eduard Delacroix' ear his own name, Mr. Jingles. He escapes death under the foot of Percy Wetmore because John Coffey was able to 'help' him. He symbolically represents that he is worthy of being alive regardless of his size or his species. A close-up of the mouse at the beginning of the film is followed by a close-up shot of John Coffey at the end.

John Coffey, played by Michael Duncan, is physically powerful, performs miracles by extracting deadly forces and expelling them through his mouth. He is characterized as a big, black idiot who is afraid of the dark and cries like a baby. Even though he is gifted with healing powers, he is compared to a mongrel dog by Mr. Detterick, the twins' father, and referred to as a "nigger" in several instances throughout the story. When John goes to cure the Warden's wife, Melinda, he ignores her reference to his "nigger cock." The Warden himself questions why Paul brings a convicted child murderer to lay hands on his wife. Stephen King described how the whole house moved when Coffey lay his mouth on Melinda, extracted her sickness and afterwards how she looked ten years younger.

Unlike the mouse, John Coffey does not consider his life worthy. John, who was described by Brutal, the prison guard, as a gift of God, wants to die. Of course he wants to die. He had already been tried and convicted in the press. He was not truthfully represented; his own lawyer didn't believe him. It took forty-five minutes to pronounce his death sentence. He was misinterpreted because of his limited knowledge of language. When he was found crying with the naked dead girls, he said, "I couldn't help it. I tried to take it back but it was too late." He meant he could not take the girls' death back because they were already dead and he found them too late. The authorities interpreted this as his confession. He gets no love and has no beauty in his life. Even after Paul Edgecombe found he could prove his innocence, Coffey was not going to get a retrial because he was a Negro. Sad work songs and piano chords signal the impending death of John Coffey, the healer, the innocent.

Paul Edgecombe's wife, Jan, pleas for John's release from his conviction. Her insistence that her husband and the other prison guards 'do something about it' was not adapted to the film version. The persuasive argument for his life was not visually promoted to a film audience. In the end, the prison guards did what they had to do. After they dispensed death to John Coffey, they were not able to take part in another execution.

The film images the characters in the book. It extracted from the book the essential qualities inherent in their personalities to represent the thematic elements of the story. One of the major themes is that one does not escape punishment for wrongdoing. Percy hated Delacroix and Delacroix' relationship with the mouse. Percy knowingly neglected to soak the sponge in brine to better conduct the charge of direct current that ran through the wire and through the sponge to Delacroix' brain. Delacroix suffered a 'bad' death and because he was not sufficiently dead, had to be electrocuted again. This sequence of actions was accompanied by thunderous booms, rumblings in the sky, lightning jabs and the visualization of clouds stacking up over a blue-colored Cold Mountain Penitentiary. Stephen King described the smell of Delacroix' death as "a devil's mixture of burned hair, fried meat and fresh baked shit." Percy was punished literally for burning Delacroix alive and the evil acts he committed toward Delacroix. By subjecting Delacroix to a 'bad' death, he suffered a mysterious wrath of punishment.

The major theme in *The Green Mile* is that if you are a person of color, you may be subjected to punishment for not committing any wrongdoing. John Coffey was convicted because of his color, his culture, and his communication. He was presumed guilty because of circumstances beyond his control.

In the film, the Fred Astaire sequence was woefully inconsistent with the characterization of John Coffey. Aside from his meal, the film states that John requested to see a film before he was executed. John is almost retarded and one of the symptoms of his mental illness is that he is very forgetful. Fred Astaire would not have any meaning for him since John is characteristically detached from earthly events. He is characterized as mystical and cannot hardly remember anything although it may have occurred a few minutes ago. This scene was out of place in the film version and it was absent in the book. One wonders why the screenwriter included it at all and why a dance sequence focusing on Fred Astaire and Ginger Rogers, in particular, was chosen to satisfy his request. Was it to depict a black man's obsessions about a white entertainer, his grace and agility which were obviously lacking in John Coffey? Was it because the screenwriter wanted to present an image of an ideal, happy, peaceful escape for John Coffey? I don't know what the answers are but he must have had to make a choice and it must have been a very difficult decision for him to create a scene that was not adapted from the book.

Paul Edgecombe's views and recollections of the year 1932 were written from a nursing home where he revisits through his narration. In the film version we only see Paul in the nursing home nearing the end of his life. The powers he received from Coffey made him resistant to aging. He is involved in a flirtatious relationship with an eighty-year old resident at the home.

The *Green Mile* is an imaginative work of literature that is substantiated by the authentic themes and language which contribute to a more explicit description of racial overtones and prejudices. Paul still refers to John, who is almost twice his size as 'boy' or his 'boy.' The visual adaptation is punctuated by sounds and images which intensifies the drama. The sounds of the lightning and rain outside the Cold Mountain Penitentiary is metaphorically related to the flashing of the electrical current and the water used to charge the electrical surge for execution.

The problem of adapting this novel of over five hundred pages was solved by extending the normal viewing film time of approximately 108 minutes to three hours. While I watched *The Green Mile*, I was not aware of the time element and I remember remarking that it did not seem like three hours to me. I actually hesitated seeing the film because I knew that the novel, which was originally produced serially in five parts was a lengthy work and that the film would probably be extensive as well. (After an hour and a half I wish most films would end.) I chose to look at *The Green Mile* after I heard the actor, Michael Clarke Duncan, who portrays John Coffey, on television encouraging people to see the film. I was also stimulated by the issues. People of color, are so hungry to see themselves depicted in larger than life settings that although some of the characteristics attributed to John Coffey were stereotypical, the overarching concern is that it was enlightening to see that Michael Clarke Duncan portrayed his character perfectly. His actions made Coffey believable.

The author, Stephen King, directly addresses his audience and in one of Paul's nursing home situations, he specifically makes a reference to the reader regarding a cable service. He warns the reader about the environment within the nursing home and in another chapter of the book, asks readers if they remember the big accident in which Paul's wife, Jan, dies. There was no such communication in the film. The format of the film diverged somewhat from the book in this respect. There were no shifts in times as those experienced by Paul Edgecombe when he revisited the nursing home intermittently throughout the narrative and chronicled the events which occurred in 1932.

The Green Mile offers many symbolic references to communicate its tonal quality. When Percy Wetmore crushed the mouse with his feet, it made a human, agonizing sound that surprised the inmates. And, after John Coffey 'helped' the mouse to regain his consciousness, the mouse limped in the same manner as the men in the penitentiary limped. This suggested to me that the inmates were beaten, or crushed as the mouse had been. Melinda Moores put the St. Christopher cross around John's neck to protect him after he 'helps' her to survive a brain tumor but the cross had no effect whatsoever on him, which symbolizes to me the uselessness of signs, symbols, or figures to save your life. And when she tells him that she dreamt of him and he found her, the concurrence on her part of the closeness between the varying levels of reality is revealed. Dreams are also part of reality. The authorities could not explain John's appearance at the site where the girls died and one person mentioned that it was as if he 'fell out of the sky.'

In *The Green Mile*, John Coffey's character doesn't even measure up to a mouse. Stephen King distributes strengths and weaknesses which are relatively comparable between these two characters and it is hard to determine which one is the more powerful. The mouse, as small as he was, had three big prison guards trying to kill him and this they were not able to do. John is physically large in stature and of gigantic proportions. The closeup of his dead face was so large; it covered the entire screen. Although he is physically and morally strong, mentally, his character is weak. He is incapable of communicating his own innocence. John Coffey in *The Green Mile* represents not only an innocent person on death row, who because of his color, culture and mental state is put to death for something he did not do, but all people of color who have no power to determine their own lives.

Existentialism & Art

Existentialism

Existentialism, the subject of being, addresses the substance and problems of human existence. It is a movement which manifested itself in the writings of Biblical man, philosophical figures, and poets and proceeded to capture the imagination of visual artists and dramatists. Existentialism is a phenomenon of thought and action that centers on the individual and one's existence. It is a matter of philosophical inquiry recognized by the attention it gives to life, living and human activity.

Existentialist themes have been explored through thought, word, religion, art and film and although France is largely responsible for giving it a voice, it is a uniquely European experience, one which drew its philosophical energies from many European thinkers, some of whom operated in radically different national traditions. Germans in the late 19th century were looking for a new interpretation of man that was made necessary by the extraordinary additions to knowledge in all of the special sciences that dealt with man. (Barrett, p. 12) The creators of existential philosophy, Martin Heidegger and Karl Jaspers, the phenomenologist Edmund Husserl, and Max Scheler were some of the Germans associated with recognizing that modern man had become very problematic. Soren Kierkegaard and Friedrich Nietzsche, whose central subject was the unique experience of the single one, the individual struggling for self-realization, in questioning Christianity and God, were considered among the greatest of intuitive psychologists in the formulation of existentialism. Martin Buber led the thinking in a desperate modern search for roots. The Russians contributed Vladimir Solovev, Leon Shestov and Nikolai Berdyaev. They brought a total, extreme and apocalyptic vision to Existentialism. Spain contributed the writer Miguel de Unamuno to the whole philosophical movement and the creative thought of Jose Ortega y Gasset.

The Sources

The primitives, early man, were existentialists because they expressed in dance, actions, movements, drawings, paintings, wood, stone and bronze sculptures, the nature of their experiences on earth. They were not at a stage in their development, however, in which an existentialist mode of communication existed that expressed this involvement with their world. Their art revealed the visual expressions of their human existence. The French poet Rimbaud was among the first of the creative artists to announce primitivism as one of the goals of his art and of his life. From Paul Gauguin to D. H. Lawrence, primitivism has been a varied and rich source. (Barrett, p. 132)

The themes of existentialism, namely, individual existence, subjectivity, freedom, truth, choice and death, had its beginnings with Hebraism, and its moral concepts and beliefs of a man of faith who is passionately committed to his own mortal being. (Barrett, p. 76) Hebrew man was secure with his trust in a spiritual entity who provided support for his existence. The Greeks questioned the absence of this entity and confronted Hebraism with critical and philosophical reflection and created their own theories of morality and idealism based on intellectual reasoning, logic, and rationalism. This was the period of Hellenism in which reason and the application of the intellect framed the scientific basis of existence. (Nietzsche, writing in the mid-19th century, for instance, asserted that the scientific assumption of an orderly universe is for the most part a useful fiction.) The technological advances made in that era demonstrated the vastness of the universe in which humans experienced isolation, detachment and alienation in relation to this limitless environment. Existentialist philosophers address the anguish, and alienation that humans experience in their inability to explain the scientific and mathematical constructs within the universe. These forces, Hebraism and Hellenism, have contributed to the field of Existentialism and philosophers since these early beginnings rely on these sources to make meaning of one's existence.

Existentialism flourished throughout the ages and contributions to this study of humanism were made by thinkers throughout the European community. Theologians and dialecticians continued to debate philosophies of faith and reason in their attempt to comprehend the nature of the universe. "Know thyself!" was the command the philosopher Socrates issued to his contemporaries in the 4th century. (Barrett, p. 4) St. Thomas Aquinas in the 13th century explored the concepts of existence and essence which were furthered by Jean Paul Sartre in his later work. Soren Kierkegaard, the 19th century philosopher generally regarded as the founder of modern existentialism, considered it a tragedy for humans to die without having touched the roots of our own existence. (Barrett, p. 3) Sartre found man rootless. Kierkegaard, a Christian, stressed the belief that one must choose one's own way without the aid of universal, objective standards and interpreted that it was God's way of calling each individual to make a commitment to a personally valid way of life. It was the German philosopher, Martin Heidegger, who in his search for self argued that the individual finds it incomprehensible why he exists and that each individual must choose a goal and follow it with passionate conviction aware of the certainty of death and the ultimate meaninglessness of one's life. Heidegger further philosophized that the individual's confrontation with nothingness, in which the impossibility of finding ultimate justification for the choices one makes, leads to further anxiety. In Heidegger's words, man is a stranger to himself. These opinions form the basis of existentialist theory.

The sources of existentialism vary because of the diversity of positions associated with existentialism. Most existential philosophers agree, however, that each individual is responsible for his or her own choices and moral decisions. In sum, existential philosophy centers on man, woman, oneself and one's relationships with and within the universe.

Existentialism and Art

Knowledge of the self, a central theme of existential inquiry, has been and continues to be represented in art. The French artist, Paul Gauguin, was probably one of the first known existentialist artists judging from the way in which he approached his work and his life. He sought to express interior states rather than surface appearances. Gauguin, was known primarily for his ability to communicate intangibles and their emotive qualities. He believed his expressive potential rested in primitive culture and when confronted with the harsh reality that the unspoiled, exotic and sensual, cultural expression he sought escaped him, he invented the world he sought, not only in paintings but with woodcarvings, graphics, and written works. As he struggled with ways to express the existential questions of life, death, knowledge and evil that preoccupied him, he interwove the images and mythology of his primitive island life with those of the West and other cultures. (Gauguin Overview, National Gallery of Art, Washington, DC 2000)

The works of Constantin Brancusi most clearly embody the essence of existentialism. His art is most visually reflective of the Hebraic/Hellenistic continuum. *The First Step* is Brancusi's first piece in wood. The influence of African carving is evident. (Geist, p. 45) Like many of his friends, he was struck by the power of African sculpture, declaring that only the Africans and Rumanians knew how to carve wood. Brancusi declaimed against the influence of African art and destroyed work where it had appeared. African sculpture had the effect of intensifying the rationalization of his forms. The aim of Brancusi's imagery is to connect rational form and essential form.

Of his *Bird in Space* Brancusi said, "I seek the essence of flight." In his study of Brancusi's work, Sidney Geist writes:

> By the clear conjunction of object and essence, avoiding resemblance which is their mutual debasement, Brancusi's later sculpture induces an effect like a flicker of the mind. Matter is spiritualized – before your eyes, as it were. The movement between that which is seen and that which is understood is like an effect of cubism. Between the data of the world and an intuition of their significance, the sculpture mediates as a sign pointing both ways. The concision of the sculpture gives rise to a euphoria of intuition. The primary experience on seeing a sculpture by Brancusi is that of knowing it at once. (Geist, p. 146)

Henri Matisse, celebrated as one of the 20th century's greatest colorists, is also now recognized for the brilliant inventions he brought to his sculptural compositions. Matisse was fascinated with the tonal dynamics of Post-Impressionism and his vivid compositions gave color an emotive, independent role. Matisse's first sculptures were created during his student years. This early sculpture reveals an interest in African art and in Rodin. (WebMuseum, Paris) Not surprisingly, his earliest figures were copies after small-scale bronzes.

The influence of African art played a major role in the development of existentialism in the visual arts in France. "Around 1900 French painters became interested in African sculpture." (Barrett, p. 46) French painters became interested in African sculpture to transact, like the poet Rimbaud, passionately and genuinely with the 'primitive, primal sources of Being and vision.' The interest shown by French painters and their contemporaries in African sculpture increased their self-perception, greatly influenced the creative activity in Paris, France, and affected the outcome of the modern art movement.

This contact with African art contributed significantly to the French existentialist art movement by broadening the scope of the artist's involvement with new mediums of creative expression. Artists found in African art themes which were consistent with their inner motivations for expressing themselves visually. African sculpture and art became a source of inspiration for exploring the artist's inner landscape. By looking at the non-intellectual, primal sources of creativity, artists were able to connect with their deepest instincts and emotions. This look inward provided a framework which was compatible with the basic foundation of existentialism, the search for self and individual expression.

African art is characterized by distinctive attributes of color, simplicity, form, pattern and abstraction. These characteristics were incorporated in the creative language of the visual artists. The initiation in African art transformed existing art concepts by reflecting the contact with the aesthetic sensibilities inherent in African art. These distinctive qualities in African art, the dramatic use of pure color, simplicity in form, flat shapes, strong patterns and abstraction, have since informed the conceptualization and production of modern art. Prior to the 1900's, French and European artists worked mainly in the tradition of classical humanism. It is no coincidence that modern art which is characterized by a break in traditional art forms, the bold use of color, abstract form, innovative and dynamic artistic presentation, and the use of non-traditional materials developed at the turn of the century.

Although not French, Pablo Picasso, born in the town of Malagna, Spain, traveled to Paris several times beginning in 1900 before settling there permanently in 1904 in Montmartre. During this time, Paris had become the center of cultural activity attracting people from all over Europe and the United States. (Sheringham and Hewitt) Artists were drawn there because of the intellectual environment inspired by the universities and the publishing houses, the inexpensive lodgings, cheap food and wine. Café culture developed throughout the 1900's as the café became more fashionable as a meeting place, discussion and entertainment center. Cafes also represented varying political traditions.

Between 1900 and 1901, Picasso's work reflected a variety of new styles and techniques, such as the introduction of bright, unmixed colors. Picasso's sculpture most noticeably exhibits the influence of African art. Attracted to the emotive power of this art, Picasso, along with Vlaminck, Matisse and Derain, began to collect masks and wood carvings as early as 1904. (Penrose, p. 18) Sculpture of Picasso bears a strong resemblance to and in similar respects derives its formal attributes from African sculpture. Some direct results of African influence in his three-dimensional work, particularly in the wood carvings, is shown in *Figure* (1907). The radical changes of style to which Picasso was exposed set him on a path that was to lead him to the discoveries of cubism, the classicism of modern art from which all modern abstract art that is valid has derived. (Barrett, p. 48)

> Like Religion, art has its miracles, and it was a miracle for Picasso, Braque, Derain, Vlaminck and Matisse to find an answer to their misgivings and, if not guidance, at least a means of breaking loose from conventional forms and re-exploring the field of plastic invention, thus opening the door – at last – to *total freedom*. (Ital. supplied; Meauze, p. 8)

Existentialism and World War II

The existentialist philosophy developed in France most rapidly after World War II. Marshal Petain headed the collaborationist Vichy government in unoccupied France, while General Charles de Gaulle led the "Free French" resistance. (Wright) The Vichy government was an extreme right-wing, anti-Semitic, racist government. The government assisted in the destruction of Jewish people by not resisting the German invasion of France and not opposing their forces and ideologies. In World War II, defeat by Germany in 1940 was followed by occupation. The occupation of France by Germany impacted on France's collective national consciousness. The crisis of the War and the experience of the French under German Occupation brought with it a real threat to life and freedom and the realization of human finitude affected the thought and philosophical discourse in this era. It was this experience that produced the thinking that expanded the course of French existential philosophy and thrust the existentialist writer Jean Paul Sartre to the forefront in the commitment of free will to create changes in the political situation.

According to Jean Paul Sartre, existence precedes essence and man has a responsibility to make his self by action and involvement. Sartre based his philosophy within an existentialist framework which centered on issues of freedom, choice, and individual commitment in this particular political situation. His philosophy was formed within the existing political climate in which freedom, a basic existential principle, was being challenged. In his writings "Why Write?" and *No Exit*, Sartre promotes his philosophy of taking responsibility for one's self and one's writings as it affects others and taking responsibility for the choices one makes.

Two works in particular which are similarly situated with respect to their form, content and structure and which are framed within the cultural context of French existentialism are Albert Camus' *L'Etranger* and Alberto Giacometti's *Femme debout II*. Although these works are drawn from different art forms, they share relationships through which an understanding of the human condition is revealed. Both works focus on solitary, individual figures interacting with their environments. These figures are alienated in terms of their conditions and their own unique experiences which they alone perceive. Each owns their own reality which although not real, exists through a transformation of thoughts by their creators. They exist *in* a sense and *out* of touch with reality. They are present but they are not here. The character in *L'Etranger*, (The Stranger) and the figure in *Femme debout II*, (Woman Standing II,) present themselves from their own points of view and are realized only through one's interpretation. They are almost human.

Albert Camus' *L'Etranger*, written during the period of German occupation of France, is a literal interpretation of existentialism. The existentialist hero in *L'Etranger* is Meursault. Meursault represents the epitome of the existentialist character, a complex individual who grapples with experiencing life on his own terms and takes responsibility for the consequences. A solitary figure, Meursault is detached from his family. His mother has just died and he reacts in his own way to her death, openly and honestly, void of tears and emotional drama.

Mother died today. Or, maybe, yesterday; I can't be sure. The telegram from the Home says: Your mother passed away. Funeral tomorrow. Deep sympathy. Which leaves the matter doubtful; it could have been yesterday. (Camus, p. 1)

The tonal quality is one of melancholy but not melodrama. Meursault, is respectfully saddened by his mother's death but not overly demonstrative of what he is experiencing. He reacted to his mother's death calmly and accepts her death as a part of the experiences that one takes part in the process of life. Meursault was truthful in his acceptance of this loss. Meursault kills someone and for this, he is sentenced to death but not because of the crime he committed, but because in the judgment of his accusers, he did not react appropriately to his mother's death. While imprisoned, Meursault experiences a loss of freedom; he has no rights.

Camus presents a tragic portrait of Meursault. He does not believe in God; he is anti-Christ. He killed someone but is hopeful for his release and since he killed *only* an Arab, he supposes he should be free. Life in prison is unbearable for him. He smells the darkness. He has no visitors, just the bugs. Not even his lawyer visits him. Meursault accepts these events almost as if they were surreal, out-of-body occurrences. Nothing really moves him. The only show of emotion Meursault made happened in court when the prosecutor was asked if he had any questions to put and he answered loudly: "Certainly not! I have all I want." His tone and the look of triumph on his face, as he glanced at Meursault, were so marked that Meursault felt as he hadn't felt for ages. He had a foolish desire to burst into tears. For the first time he realized how all these people loathed him. (Camus, p. 112) And Camus, in an extraordinary display of literary persuasion encourages the reader to sympathize with him, his conflicts and his fate. Meursault made choices, however, which contributed to his downfall and even though he was sentenced to death for the wrong reasons, he still fictionally had to take responsibility for the actions of taking someone's life.

The Stranger also deals with another branch of existentialist theory that recognizes the absurdity of life. Camus further explores the issue of absurdity in the *Myth of Sisyphus* in which he questions how and why circumstances in life are presented to, for example, Meursault. In *Myth*, Camus finally concludes that the point of life is 'to live' because we do not have the answers to those questions and that true knowledge is impossible to attain.

Camus in *The Stranger* presents existentialist themes of freedom, choice, death, individuality, and inner emotions unaccompanied by the usual climaxes, dynamic stylization, and literary values that are traditionally associated with literature. The structure is not dramatic; it is leveled, flat. There is no definitive beginning, middle or end. The temporal order of the narrative is vague as the element of time is equally distributed throughout the novel. Meursault is situated on a vast open page that suggests an infinity of unwritten space. His story has no end.

In 1922, Swiss born Alberto Giacometti came to France and continued to work within the existentialist milieu. He conveyed in his paintings and sculpture, the spiritual essence of humanity and tried to show his perception of reality in these objects. Giacometti's *Femme debout II*, (*Woman Standing II*,) a thin, weightless, bronze sculpture, completed during the years 1959-60 visually mirrors the literary figure Meursault in Camus' *The Stranger*. *Woman Standing II* reflects the sense of alienation, despair and isolation, experienced by Meursault in and out of prison and his total lack of control over his life. Standing, over 12' tall, her proportions are distorted and her facial image is physically out of view. She is almost faceless; her features are unrecognizable. Her form is vague and the outline is uneven. The bronze texture of this vertical sculptural figure is rough indicating that like Meursault, complications, problems, are under its surface.

Woman Standing II was made to be placed in a very large space to distance the sculpture from the viewer. Ironic, defiant, ceremonious and tender, Giacometti sees empty space everywhere. (Refers to statements published in *Les Temps Modernes*, June, 1954, concerning an exhibition of paintings by Giacometti at the Galerie Maeght.) Giacometti creates a vacuum, the environment, in which the figure stands but it is a kind of circular distance. The form is complete with the space. Because the whole space is important to the presentation of *Woman*, the whole space is valued in relation to the sculpture. Both the sculpture and the space are equally important and share the same value. Within this space dimension, *Woman Standing II* is lost. She is so small in this space, it is as if she is not there. Although distanced, it is endowed with a 'presence' that Giacometti conveys in his placement of the sculpture. In relation to the size of her environment *Woman* is indistinguishable. Giacometti wanted to convey an extreme loss of identity and stability with this structure and in that position, *Woman Standing II* is a piece of 'nothing.' (from statements in *Les Temps Modernes*)

Giacometti's work parallels the literary composition by Albert Camus. *Woman Standing II* represents the existentialist, the individual. The image of a totem is recognized in *Woman* and it was the artist's intention to render the timelessness and eloquence of ancient sculpture in its entirety. Giacometti believed that he could express 'the totality of life' in his installations and this was a recurrent theme in works created by him in later years.

The Legacy of Existentialism

Throughout the 1950's and 60's existential themes were represented in all areas of artistic communication throughout the world. The American artist Alexander Calder found Josephine Baker, who personified the essential free spirit, a rich source with which to symbolize his association with French existentialism. Samuel Beckett wrote "Waiting for Godot," a philosophically challenging work which examines existential issues of an indifferent universe and the crisis of faith. In this play, Beckett explores the individual's interaction with God and questions God's existence. In the play, *Godot*, Godot may be interpreted as God, who exists, but is not seen. Beckett wrestles with faith and belief in relation to rationalization. The characters, Estragon and Vladimir, in "Waiting for Godot" 'wait' but Godot never appears. Waiting further indicates our 'outsideness' in nature. We have to wait and nature is the constant being, the ever-present operative, to which man has to conform and over which man has no influence. Waiting, as Martin Esslin posits in "The Theatre of the Absurd," is an essential and characteristic aspect of the human condition.

Christian existentialism was explored by Robert Bresson in the film "A Man Escaped." Bresson involves the viewer in a suspenseful drama of Fontaine's and Jost's escape from prison. Although a level of reality is present, Bresson, creates a transcendental element of spirituality with dramatic light and dark images, intriguing shadows and an exciting interplay of these visual effects. This element reveals a supernatural aura in Bresson's filmmaking. Bresson masterfully combines sounds and silence, movement and stillness, active and reflective stances to convey the plot of the film. The film is held together tightly in terms of its intense interaction with the themes and attention to the framework of Christian existentialism. Allen Thiher in the *Cinematic Muse* literally contextualizes this film within the existentialist philosophy. He points to Fontaine's expression of will to escape, his determination, his trust in the prisoner Terry, his responsibility for his freedom and leap of faith, the final act to be free.

Francois Truffaut's "The Four Hundred Blows" is representative of the New Wave in modern filmmaking which occurred in post-war France. Filmmakers in New Wave cinema were concerned more with their personal forms of expression which led to the development of auteur theory. Filming in open spaces on location as opposed to filming in the studio, new techniques (films were made in the day and filters were used to create the night shots,) spontaneity and improvisation were utilized in the creation of New Wave film. "The Four Hundred Blows" reflect the existentialist sensibility of freedom, nature, individualism and leap of faith. The main character, Antoine escaped from the juvenile detention home and fled to the sea. Through the attention of the camera and sound, the psychological reasons why Antoine is alienated from his parents and the world are revealed. The camera records every movement of his flight and then freeze frames him to portray his entrapment, devastation and seclusion from the outside world. Truffaut, in this filmic episode reminds us that we are still bound by circumstances beyond control but that we still have to bear responsibility for the choices we make.

The influence of Existentialism continues to be evidenced in the approach that artists bring to their work. Poetry once conceived to be a formal means of expression has been freed from its basic rhythmic structure. The poet is free to experiment with new modes of expression in a field of openness or nothingness. Writers have created a new vocabulary for communicating their personal attitudes and ideas and artists have been freed to create outside the frame. Installations dominate contemporary exhibitions and challenge the very notion of art. The ritual in dance has been restored and presents itself in works of modern dance and performance art. Existentialism has been transplanted in the depths of the human experience and has provided a philosophy with which to create and give voice and meaning to being in our world.

BIBLIOGRAPHY

William Barrett, *Irrational Man*, Doubleday & Company, 1958

Albert Camus, *The Stranger*, Librairie Gallimard, 1942

Sidney Geist, *Brancusi*, Grossman Publishers, 1967

Pierre Meauze, *African Art*, Meulenhoff International, 1968

National Gallery of Art, *Gauguin Overview*, Washington, DC 2000

Roland Penrose, *The Sculpture of Picasso*, The Museum of Modern Art, 1967

Michael Sheringham, *Parisian Fields*, Nicholas Hewitt Shifting Cultural Centers in 20th Century Paris, Reaktion Books, 1966

Papers, WebMuseum, Paris

Gordon Wright, *France in Modern Times*, W. W. Norton Company, Inc. 1981

"One Love"
One Long Love Story

"One Love"
One Long Love Story
1970

I met Carlton Barrington Ingleton at a wedding reception for my first boyfriend, Patrick Creary. Pat and I never had sex. When I met Pat, I was only about fourteen and not only scared of having sex but scared of getting pregnant. When I did have sex for the first time, I was over eighteen. I made sure I was out of high school and had a job. I had to tell you that because even Carl thought I had sex with Pat and I don't think Carl believed me. Believe what you want to believe. I know my own truth. Anyway this is not about Pat or my sex life. This is about Carlton and our love life. Carlton saw my graduation picture at Pat's house and told me he either fell in love with me or my picture. I can't remember which one.

The first time I saw Carlton, I was impressed. He was tall, black, and just like his father, had blue eyes (yes, real blue eyes), a nice big face, wide forehead, high cheekbones, big lips, big nose and so cool. I loved him. He was beautiful. He asked me to dance. He also asked me to go to an after-party with him and I said, "No." How can I go anywhere with you? I am with my sisters and I just met you. I did give him my number and when he called, he invited me to his sister's house for dinner and I went but couldn't find the apartment. We did eventually have a first date and that was probably our last. We went to see a movie of his choice, of course, one with Frank Sinatra, something about Oceans. I can't remember the title of the movie. I should have known then that things were going to go his way but he was so fine, a man, a real man with muscles, kind-hearted, a good man, a sweet-talker and talented. I saw a portrait he created of His Imperial Majesty Haile Selassie and knew he was exceptionally talented and I told him so. I was in awe. My mother was a painter and painted very well but she always considered herself an amateur. Carlton was a fine artist, a painter and sculptor and he could make things with his hands, boxes, beds, furniture and everything he touched was 'perfect.' And not only that, he had a job; he worked in construction.

The first time I went to his apartment, he said he would cook for me and I thought we were going to watch TV. His apartment was immaculate. I made about three steps in and I was on my back. Five minutes later he told me we were going to get married. I kept thinking I must be in love. The bed he made was stationed by the front door in his studio apartment. He called it a captain's bed and we slept on that 3'+x6'+ bed for years even after he told me he never asked me to marry him. You ****! I was pregnant and we were getting married! And everything is going to be fine! We both cook, clean, and work. Later on, I would tell my sons, "Don't lay down with someone who you would not want to marry."

Not too long after we met, Carlton started going to the Art Students League. It was only natural that he study what he was best at. He loved the League – life models, the freedom to be an artist, and the people who all shared the same creative desires. I supported the family, and since he no longer worked in construction, he worked freelancing, making storefront signs, lettering, creating jewelry, and graphic designs. Carl was free to do his work and that was all he wanted to do. He was a little like my father, got up early, and went to work. We eventually founded the 843 Studio Gallery, a not-for-profit cultural arts organization to exhibit and promote his work and the work of community artists. We worked very well together and our life was good. We had a common interest in art and my experience in dance and art administration solidified our relationship. We were the best of friends. I felt like he was my brother.

The day we got married, I found out Carlton was ten years older than I. I was twenty-two and I just assumed that he was a couple of years older. He really looked good and much younger. The day we got married, the day, August 18, 1972, he told me he was not going to cook anymore. He had me, a wife. The day we got married, he drove to North Carolina or South Carolina (it could have been Virginia) and told me he couldn't make love to me because he was too tired from driving and I understood but I couldn't understand why we had to go all the way to North Carolina or South Carolina for him to tell me that. We could have stayed at home. The day we got married, I knew that things were changing very quickly but my love never changed. I was in love for ever. Our relationship grew and we made three children together and Carl, even though he didn't always do the right thing, he meant to. I loved Carl because he was disciplined and he loved to create his artwork. I loved Carl because he loved our children and he loved our family. I loved Carl because he loved me and I know he loved me. I have all the love letters he wrote to me.

Art was first in Carlton's life. He was always worrying about his family and felt that creating art was the best way he could give us a good life. He suffered with depression. We wanted him to spend more time with us and not work so much. He worked every day. I would tell him, "Carl I think we should have one day where we can get together as a family, just us, no work." He said, "No." We never went out to dinner as a family. He didn't like to eat out and we ate at home. I did most of the cooking until I got my sons, to cook. No matter how much food I made, they wanted more. Then Carl told them that they were "men" and did not have to wash dishes. I told them if they didn't wash dishes, they couldn't eat. I told them if they didn't wash dishes, they couldn't live with me and one of my sons did leave and go to my sister's house. He came back when he found out if you eat in someone's house you eventually have to wash dishes. He decided to wash dishes in his own house.

I washed most of the dishes anyway, did most or all of the housework, worked at NYU, paid the rent and most of the bills, and administered the Gallery's programs. For two years, there was something wrong with the sink and I had to wash dishes in two large aluminum bins and nobody remembers that phase because no one else washed dishes. Eventually I was washed out. Why wasn't the kitchen sink fixed? Carl didn't want management to come into our apartment. Why? Maybe it was because he smoked ganja morning, noon and night. Carlton was a Rastafarian and when I asked why he smoked so much, he said, "I don't smoke more than the average Jamaican." Carl was very good with the words. And because he didn't want management to come into the apartment, for over twenty years I did not have a light in my dining room near the kitchen and that made me upset – for over twenty years. But guess what, I loved him and I put up with a lot to keep the marriage together and we lived together for over thirty years.

Don't think for one minute our marriage was easy. It was good but it wasn't easy. The kids in our arts program had a name for us. They called us the Huxtables. Everyone thought we were the ideal family! We were, ideally! We did have great times and a lot of fun together! Individually, we had issues, Carlton wanted us, all of us, to do what he wanted us to do. He was the man and he was the eldest. That was not going to work for all of us. I proposed that if individual needs were met, we would work better as a family. Carlton's mottos were, 'Family First,' 'The Family That Works Together Stays Together,' and 'Working Together For The Family.' We got the message – work.

Carlton, for one, framed his life within the Rastafarian philosophy expounding on the life and works of His Imperial Majesty Haile Selassie, the quotes of Marcus Garvey and the musical genius of Bob Marley. When sculpting, he moved his hammer and chisel to the beat of Bob's. When socializing, he would engage his contemporaries in, aside from art, two of his favorite topics, religion and politics, and even though he always maintained no one had to disclose their religious or political views, he openly promoted his. Carlton was an early riser and of course, we all had to rise early. These early risings would eventually lead to discussions about religion and politics which Carl would dominate. My sons were drawn to the Hebrew way of life which Carl would not entertain. He told me I had to get down on my knees and pray every night and even though I told him I prayed to my God everyday and sometimes all day, that was not enough for him. I got down on my knees and prayed every night. I did it. It didn't hurt me.

When in January 2001, I asked Carl "Can you be a little more affectionate with me?" and he said, "No," that was 'the straw that broke the camel's back.' He said, "That's not my thing. I hope you find someone." Find someone? I'm not looking for anyone. I want you. After all these years of begging for attention, affection, time and patience and after all these years of making you happy, you won't even try to treat me like a woman. He was happy. I did everything to make Carl happy. He always credited me with contributing to his livelihood and he always told me he loved me. He just didn't know how to show it and he didn't want to learn. I do everything for you and you don't do anything for me. You never complained about me. You said you ate very well and that I was a great baker. You said I was the best wife – the best mother! I didn't know who I was anymore. I gave myself to you. I was lost!

Eight months later, when I left him to find myself, I was approaching my fifty-first birthday. I stopped getting down on my knees to pray. I stood up, lifted my hands up, and prayed to my God to bless me forever and to give me the strength to live and survive on my own. I survived. I slept on my daughter's couch for six months until she moved and handed the apartment over to me. The apartment she was living in was in my name. I was getting accustomed to living on my own.

It was not easy for me to move away from Carlton. He was my husband. I loved him and I knew he loved me. I had left him once before about three years after we were married. I went to my mother's house but he wouldn't leave me alone. He bought Al Green's song or album, *Let's Stay Together* for me; he called me every morning and every night. He needed me and he was not happy when I was not there. One day I came to visit him and I saw him take out food from a Chinese restaurant on Utica Avenue and I was really worried. He hated Chinese food (when the Chinese restaurant opened up across the street from the Gallery, we were forbidden to go there) and I knew he was smoking and not eating well. I didn't want him to go crazy again. The first time he went crazy, was before my first daughter was born. I knew he was stressed with the new one coming and worried about how he was going to provide for the family. He smoked and read the Bible constantly. He thought he was God's son. My mother told him to put down the bible, stop smoking and eat some food. He cursed my mother maliciously! He told me he wanted his son and I can take my daughter and the kids would have to split up. I came back home – to make him happy, to keep him sane and to keep my family together. I had no regrets. I did the right thing. The one time, one time, we had relations in one month, I was blessed with my third child. Neither Carl nor I could believe it. Believe it. It happened. When I said to the doctor, "We only did it once." The doctor said, "That's all it takes, one time." I knew I did the right thing.

This time, I wasn't coming back. I made my mind up. It was no coincidence that when I left, my youngest son was twenty-one. Our middle son was almost twenty-five and working and our eldest daughter was twenty-eight, married and had one child. She left our house when she was sixteen because Carlton hit her. I didn't find out about that until much later. I assumed she left because Carl did not separate the room she shared with her brothers and she needed privacy. I was wrong. He threatened me that something would happen to me for leaving him and I thought the sky would fall on me. It didn't and I was doing alright.

As a family we were still very committed and devoted to each other. I promised Carl that I would be married to him forever and I kept my promise to this day. I never divorced my husband and he didn't divorce me. We still worked together because we worked together very well. We met often and I still cooked for the family at times. He started working as an instructor at Medgar Evers. I helped him with his syllabus, course materials, the student exhibitions at the Gallery and even taught his class at Medgar Evers one day. As he was approaching his sixty-seventh year, we finally convinced him to relax and we started working together to establish a Café in connection with the Gallery, a meeting place for artists and the community. Two weeks before he died, he told me he wanted to beat me. Two weeks later, he died.

"I love you but you are not going to take advantage of me."

Those were the words I told my husband the Saturday before he died. I do everything for you but you won't do anything for me. Tuesday morning, January 16, 2007, Carlton and my son, after one of their discussions, got into a 'holy war.' When my son said, "He was coming after me 'like a demon' and I had to hit him to make him stop," I believed him. When he said 'like a demon,' I knew what he meant. I had seen that look before when Carl tried to knock me down in the Gallery for buying the kids fish burgers one Friday, the one day I do not like to cook after work. When I decided that I was not going down by myself, I didn't stop until I dragged him down to the floor with me. No one, no one, is going to take advantage of me. We all loved Carlton but he wasn't easy. He was a human being and like all of us, he was not perfect.

In the end, Carlton lost his life and my son lost his mind. My son was charged with his father's death and spent almost two years in Rikers, on medication, before the court found that he was not responsible for Carlton's death or anything that happened that day. The defense, the prosecution, the forensic psychiatrists, and the court believed my son. He was taken off Zyprexa and is now in therapy at the Manhattan Psychiatric Center where he is working and is getting paid.

When you love someone, you don't ever stop loving that one – that's the way love is! Carlton was my husband. I loved him and lived with him longer than his parents, his brothers and his sisters. I loved him and I know he loved me. I took care of him. I slept with him, even when he got chicken pox and looked so awful even the doctor didn't know by looking at him what was wrong. I comforted him. I protected him. I did everything to keep my marriage together.

After all of this, three children and seven grandchildren later, some people think I had something to do with Carlton's death. Some people are evil! Some people are hateful! Some people should not say things they do not know anything about! Carlton's cousin called me on the phone and told me, "You and your son killed my cousin." I told him, "That is not true. But you know what, I will pray for you. I pray that you see the light." I cannot conceive of killing someone who I love and I know my son loved his father very much. His cousin wrote me a hateful letter in which he said I buried Carlton in a 'matchbox.' These words hurt me very much. I buried my husband the best way I could. You will see. [(www.moreculture. com); Spotlight; Carlton Ingleton] I told some people at Medgar Evers, on the evening of Carlton's Memorial, "Leave my marriage alone!" You did not live with Carl. You don't know him like I do. You do not love him like I do. No one can tell me how to conduct my marriage. No one can tell me when to stay or when to go. This is my marriage. You will never be able to understand what happened between us – you weren't there.

I promised Carl that I would be married to him through death and to this day, I kept my promise. I am a keeper.

Carlton and his first son, Carl Ossawa